器皿　多以塗金或以銀　而以靑陶器爲貴

"While most of the vessels are gilded or made from silver,
Those most valued are celadon wares."

— From "Banquet ceremony" in *Goryeo dogyeong* (高麗圖經, Illustrated Account of Goryeo)

Cheongja

Korean Traditional Celadon

Korean Craft & Design Resource Book 12

Ministry of Culture, Sports and Tourism
Korea Craft & Design Foundation

Notes to Readers

- *Cheongja: Korean Traditional Celadon* is published as part of the "Publishing Project of the Korean Craft & Design Resource Book Series" launched by the Ministry of Culture, Sports, and Tourism and developed by the Korea Craft & Design Foundation.
- All Korean terms are transliterated preferably according to the Official Romanization of Korean, excluding North Korean place names and terminology, and widely used Chinese characters are also used. Terminologies are largely based on the Korean Standard Dictionary compiled by the National Institute of the Korean Language; in some cases, terminologies used by master artisans are added with interpretations.
- Photographs in this book were taken by Seo Heun-gang and Seon Yu-min, unless indicated otherwise.

From the Publisher

The Korean Craft & Design Resource Book series published by the Korea Craft & Design Foundation is intended to systematize knowledge and information on Korean traditional craft technology, enabling both experts from related fields and general readers to easily understand and utilize it. The 2017 publication of *Cheongja: Korean Traditional Celadon* and *Ottchil: Korean Traditional Lacquer* were preceded by that of *Najeon: The Korean Nacre Lacquerware*; *Traditional Natural Dyeing*; *Somok: The Korean Traditional Joinery*; *Jangseok: The Korean Traditional Metalwork for Joinery*; *Hanji: The Korean Handmade Paper*; *Baekja: Korean Traditional Porcelain*; *Nubi: Korean Traditional Quilt*; *Onggi: Korean Traditional Earthenware*; *Chimseon: Korean Traditional Sewing*; *Maedeup: Korean Traditional Decorative Knotting*; and *Ipsa: Korean Traditional Silver or Gold Inlaying*.

In Korea, celadon (*cheongja*) began to be created since the early Goryeo period with the imported Chinese techniques of celadon production; however, by the twelfth century, Goryeo came to make celadon with a sophisticated and exquisite *bisaek* (翡色, jade-green color) that was admired by China. The publication of *Cheongja: Korean Traditional Celadon* owes much to the extensive discussions among many experts who participated in the project to facilitate a broader understanding of the value of Korean celadon, and introduce its reassessed value to the general public. The Korea Craft & Design Foundation hopes that the publication of this book will enhance understanding of the past and present of Korean celadon and stimulate the modernization of Korean celadon. I would like to extend my sincere gratitude to all those who have contributed to the successful publication of this book, including title holders and learners of Important Intangible Cultural Property of Ceramic Making, ceramic artists, museum staff, a team of writers and editors who devoted themselves to the publication even under the most difficult conditions, and the advisory panel that pointed out errors and provided explicit explanations. I sincerely hope that this book will allow craftsmen, designers, and those who are interested in Korean arts and crafts to appreciate afresh the lasting value of Korean celadon.

December 2017
Choi Bong-hyun, President of Korea Craft & Design Foundation

Recommending This Book

The beauty and technology of Goryeo Celadon

Goryeo celadon was long admired for its sophisticated form and distinctive beautiful blue color. In around the tenth century, when celadon was first made, it was difficult to control the fire because at the time vessels were fired only one time in Chinese-style kilns constructed with large bricks. Also, because oxygen was not supplied or blocked efficiently in the kiln, celadon wares displayed an olive green (greenish brown) color.

However, as celadon production developed in earnest in the Gangjin area in the eleventh century, celadon began to yield a jade color. This change occurred due to the use of a traditional Korean kiln that was small in size and constructed with mud. The use of a small kiln of 10 meters or less enabled efficient control of the fire. Therefore, it was made possible to produce celadon wares in a reduction atmosphere.

In addition, celadon wares were bisque fired at a low temperature in order to enhance the adhesion of the glaze and to filter out damaged wares. Also, bisque firing enabled thick application of the glaze. Further, their walls were built thinly, thus giving the celadon wares a light and sleek appearance. Some high-quality wares were supported on silica spurs inside the kiln, thus creating flawless works.

The completion of the green color celadon, which had attracted attention in China since the twelfth century, is based on technological power that efficiently controlled the fire in small kilns through elaborate molding and bisque firing. This tradition, of course, changed according to the trend of the times, but basically it continued until the Goryeo period.

During the golden age of Goryeo celadon, it was decorated with diverse techniques, including incising, impressing, paste-on-paste, inlaying, and underglaze iron. Furthermore, it was decorated with and made in the shape of animals, plants, and landscapes. In particular, *sanghyeong* celadon, which is modelled after certain objects and remains extant only in small numbers, demonstrates the high level of craftsmanship of Goryeo celadon.

There may be different viewpoints in understanding Korea's celadon. Readers are invited to acquire a basic knowledge of celadon in this book, which is divided into chapters of concept of celadon, production techniques, decoration techniques, and usage. Particularly in "Enjoying Korean Celadon", reference images of celadon have been well-selected, demonstrating the formative characteristics of the celadon and also displaying its beauty and elegance. Further, the book is very informative in that it explains in detail the tools, facilities, and production stages of making celadon with abundant reference images. Through this book, I hope readers will better understand the history and beauty of Korea's celadon and rediscover its charm which had blossomed through technical advancement of crafts.

December 2017

Jang Nam-won

Associate Professor, Dept. of Art History, Ewha Womans University

Director of the Museum of Ewha Womans University

Preface

The development of pottery was a hugely significant event in human history — to the extent that it has been referred to as the "Neolithic Revolution." Those who used pottery from the distant past were aware of the disadvantages and advantages of the pottery for storing and transporting, and the efforts of humankind who were seeking water-impermeable porcelain wares were first rewarded in China.

Celadon was first manufactured in China, but the celadon made in Goryeo, Korea, the second country to produce celadon, had reached a remarkable status that it was even widely admired in China.

Cheongja: Korean Traditional Celadon captures the understandings of the "celadonists" of the Goryeo Dynasty, and how these celadon traditions are handed down to our current generation. To make it easier to understand, this book provides the details of celadon production process divided into four chapters as below with reference images that were taken on sites:

Chapter 1, "Korean Celadon: Introduction" introduces the concept, the type, the use, and the history of celadon. In addition to the definition of celadon, its characteristics are introduced in the concept part, and the types of the celadon are classified into 11 kinds according to the decoration technique. And in the usage section, the celadon is examined from a practical and artistic point of view. Finally, we look at the history of Goryeo celadon and its development process in history, and discuss not only the production of celadon but also the aspects of its consumption and distribution.

Chapter 2, "Materials and Tools for Making Celadon" contains celadon material (clay body), celadon pigment, celadon glaze, workshop facilities and tools, kiln and firing tools. This chapter has been completed with detailed photographs from the materials required for the production of celadon to the production environment as well as component analysis data.

Chapter 3, "Making Celadon," introduces the celadon production process from raw-material preparation, to firing, and to finishing. The preparation raw materials include collecting, levigating, and kneading clay. In the next step of shaping, celadon vessels are modelled and their feet are trimmed. Further, the leather-hard dried celadon vessels are decorated by techniques such as incising, mold-impressing, openwork, inlaying, underglaze painting in iron brown, and paste-on-paste. Next, after firing at 900°C, the celadon vessels are glazed and second fired.

In Chapter 4, "Enjoying Korean Celadon," celadons made and used in various ways during the Goryeo period are classified into three categories: "Goryeo's Noble Taste and Elegance;" "Goryeo Celadon for Tea Drinking;" "Jade-colored Celadon, the Best under Heaven;" "Inlaid Celadon, Quintessence of Goryeo Celadon;" "Celadon with Poetry;" and "Lifelike *Sanghyeong* Celadon." Finally, we will examine how Goryeo celadon is currently being reproduced and reinterpreted through the works of contemporary ceramic artists.

This book includes the concept of celadon and the lives of those who used it. Celadon is not something from the past, but continues to be produced until now. Also, as with all cultural properties, celadon also plays a role of the medium that connects past life and culture to the present. We can read the stories of people from the past through a single piece of cultural asset. This is a compact, introductory book on celadon, but we have tried to deliver not only the essentials for a better understanding of celadon, but also the voice of the people who lived and used celadon in their respective eras. We sincerely hope that these intentions and efforts will be conveyed to our esteemed readers.

Contents

Chapter 4.
Enjoying Korean Celadon

Appendix

Chapter 1

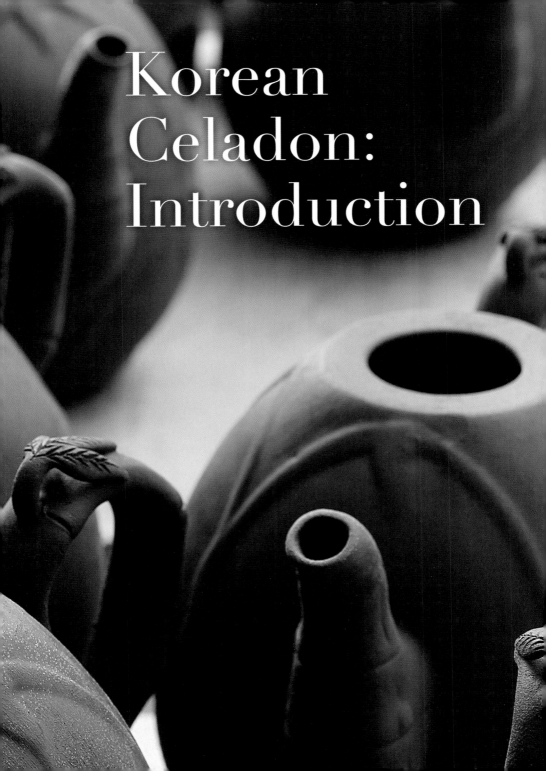

Korean Celadon: Introduction

Definition of Celadon

What is Celadon?

Celadon, or *cheongja* (青磁, meaning "green ware") in Korean, is a type of ceramic made from iron-containing clay, which is finely strained, shaped, fired, covered with glaze containing 2-3% of iron, and then fired for a second time at a high temperature of around 1,250°C. (Recent studies have revealed that some old celadon wares were fired at a temperature below 1,200°C.) Celadon is named after a green glaze applied to the surface of ceramic ware; however, colors of celadon vary according to components of clay and glaze,

Celadon Bowl with Impressed Peony Scroll Design, Goryeo, 12th century, H. 5.9cm, National Museum of Korea

the temperature inside the kiln throughout the firing, and oxidation or reduction firing techniques. As iron contained in the clay and glaze reacts during firing, reduced flames lead to the production of bluish green color, and firing with oxidized flames, yellowish green or yellowish brown.

Since its early days, the Goryeo Dynasty began producing celadon, using the imported Chinese manufacturing technique of celadon, and by the 12th century, Goryeo came to make celadon with a sophisticated and gorgeous jade-green hue, or *bisaek* (翡色, meaning "jade color") which was something that China admired.

Celadon *Maebyeong* with Inlaid Crane and Cloud Design, Treasure No. 1869, Goryeo, late 12th century, H. 30.3cm, National Museum of Korea
This is a classic example of mid-Goryeo *maebyeong*, or prunus vase, decorated with inlaid designs. This is a flawless piece with an elegant form, vibrant design, jade-colored glaze and is preserved in a good condition. This is rather small for a *maebyeong* but in a balanced form and proportion. This is an outstanding example of the 12th century *maebyeong* with gentle curves on the body from the mouth to shoulders and waist. But what is most notable in this vase is the inlaid decoration. The upper and lower ends of the vase are encircled with inlaid fret design in black, and the rest of body is inlaid with cranes and clouds at rare intervals that appear to be flying in blue skies. They look spirited and poetic at the same time.
The designs are mainly inlaid in white with some details in black. A type of jade-color glaze is applied and was fired in reduction atmosphere. It is vitrified uniformly and yields a beautiful hue. This is preserved in a flawless state.

Characteristics of Goryeo Celadon

China was the first country to produce high-fired ceramics in world history and has produced them ever since through the vast eons of time. Goryeo was the second country in the world producing and using celadon after China. Around the 13th century, some Southeast Asian countries created glazed ware similar to celadon; however, they did not succeed in making porcelaneous celadon. Japan also failed to establish its own celadon culture, and by the 17th century came to experience white porcelain culture. Although currently dominating the ceramic industry, European countries had not yet discovered the secret of making celadon or porcelain and were unable to imagine that they could enjoy the culture of celadon until the 18th century.

Goryeo celadon represents several notable achievements in the history of ceramics: the perfection of producing jade-green celadon, the distinctive

Celadon *Maebyeong* with Inlaid Plum Blossom, Bamboo, and Crane Design, Treasure No. 903, Goryeo, 12th-13th century, H. 38.9cm, private collection, managed at the National Museum of Korea
This is a typical example of Goryeo *maebyeong*, or a prunus vase, with broad shoulders and a slim waist below the body. It has a short neck and mouth. It features picturesque decoration displaying thin branches of plum blossoms, large bamboo, and birds in between them. The clear glaze yields a light bluish green hue.

Celadon Lidded Case with Inlaid Lotus Scroll Design, Goryeo, 12th century, H. 5.9cm, National Museum of Korea
This is a cylindrical case with a lid. The body is inlaid in white with alternating upright and inverted lotus flowers against the background of black-inlaid scrolls. The top of the lid is decorated with chrysanthemums inside the roundel at the center, which is surrounded by a band of lotus scrolls. The lid's brim is stamped with chrysanthemums.

decoration technique of inlaying, or *sanggam* (象嵌), and the copper-red produced with a reduction firing technique. The color of well-made Goryeo celadon was called *bisaek* (翡色, jade-green color) as it was similar to that of jade. Even Chinese people known to have made the earliest celadon wares praised *bisaek* as the "best under heaven." As a ceramic type produced second in the world after Chinese celadon, Goryeo celadon was a representative cultural legacy of the Goryeo Dynasty that embodied the artistic spirit of culturally advanced Korean ancestors. Even though China first made celadon, Goryeo developed celadon with originality and creativity, crossing the threshold of new celadon culture. China's recognition of Goryeo celadon's superiority demonstrated that Goryeo created the world's best celadon in deed as well as in name.

Celadon Gourd-shaped Ewer and Saucer with Inlaid Grapes and Boys Design in Underglaze Copper-red, Goryeo, 12th-13th century, H. 36.1, National Museum of Korea
This is a rather slim gourd-shaped ewer and a bowl with a flaring foot. The ewer is entirely covered with inlaid designs of grapes and boys playing in vines. Boys are black inlaid on the outline and so are the grapes. Some grapes are colored in copper-red. Glaze is opaque and light green colored. Some parts of the body have turned brown by oxidation. It is possible that it was made at Yucheon-ri kiln in Boan-myeon, Buan-gun, North Jeolla Province.

Types of Celadon

There are different types of celadon according to their decoration techniques.

Plain Celadon

Plain celadon generally refers to undecorated ones, but it can also include celadon wares with incised, mold-impressed, raised decorations, as well as those in openwork and modeled after certain physical shapes called *sanghyeong* celadon. From the beginning of celadon production to its demise, this type ranked highest in number, representing Goryeo celadon. Plain celadon in the prime of the 12th century pursued a flawless, pure color of jade-green and an elegant form suitable for the color.

Celadon Lobed Dish, Mid-Goryeo, H. 3cm,
Goryeo Celadon Museum
This is a dish in the shape of a fully blossomed flower. It has a wide and flat inner bottom and 12 lobes. Its surface is smooth because it is shaped with refined clay. The glazed surface yields a gray-green hue. There are three refractory spur marks on the foot suggesting that it is a high-quality ware. Silica clay kiln spurs were used to minimize the areas of glaze melted and stuck on the kiln floor.

Celadon Cup and Stand, Goryeo,12th century,
H. 5cm (cup) / 4.2cm (stand), National Museum of Korea
This is a classic example of a Goryeo celadon cup and stand. The cup rests on the stand with a tall foot, a wide rim, and an inverted-cup-shaped center. They are both coated thick with a gray-green colored glaze. The glaze displays a soft gloss and has no crackles. They are left plain yet appear very sophisticated and mature thanks to the glaze and simple form.

Celadon with Incised Decoration

Incised celadon is produced using the most fundamental and simplest technique that required engraving fine lines of designs on the surface with a graving tool. In the early stage of celadon production, undecorated celadon wares were produced the most, and starting around the 11th century, celadon wares began to be adorned with incising technique. Various designs were delicately carved, giving a subdued and refined feeling. In particular, scrolls and sprays of peonies and lotus flowers were the favored designs.

Celadon Square Dish with Incised Peony Design, Goryeo, 12th century, H. 1.7cm, National Museum of Korea
It is a square dish with four corners indented by hand. It is rather shallow. The dish is entirely decorated with incised designs. The glaze is applied thick overall, so it also yields a rather uniform color.

Celadon Octagonal Bottle with Incised Lotus Design, Treasure No. 1454, Goryeo, 12th century, H. 34.4cm, Horim Museum
This bottle has an elongated round body and a long, slim neck that is faceted into eight sides. Each of the eight facets is incised with lotus sprays in full blossom. The simple form, elaborate design, and soft green-blue glaze are well-coordinated.

Celadon with Raised Decoration

Celadon decorated in relief is produced by carving out the background of the design or impressing molds. Designs created in relief appear richer than those made by incising, so more ornate designs were used for adorning relief wares. The use of molds facilitated the mass production of celadon, and roof-end tiles are typical examples of celadon with raised decoration. According to the *History of Goryeo* (高麗史, Goryeosa), a pavilion named *Yangyijeong* (養怡亭) with celadon roof tiles was built in 1157. Celadon roof-end tiles used in actual buildings, as recorded in *Goryeosa*, are adorned with refined designs of peonies and scrolls in relief, signifying Goryeo's cultural maturity.

Celadon Incense Burner with Impressed Ferocious Animal Design, Goryeo, 12th century, H. 11.1cm, National Museum of Korea
During the Goryeo period, celadon incense burners were made after the ancient Chinese bronze cauldron called *ding* (鼎). Ding-shaped incense burners are classified into round- or square-shape. This is square-shaped, and it features panels on the body created by adhering rectangular clay slabs, short legs, and upright ears. Fret patterns are incised on the entire body. One-legged phoenix and ferocious animals decorated in relief on the upper and lower ends respectively.

(left) Celadon Roof-end Tile with Peony Design in Relief, Goryeo, 12th century, Diam. 8.3cm, L. 29.9cm, National Museum of Korea
(right) Celadon Concave Roof-end Tile with Scroll Design in Relief, Goryeo, 12th century, H. 4.1cm, L. 26.4cm, W. 19.9cm, National Museum of Korea
As Buddhism flourished during the Goryeo Dynasty, temples were built in vast numbers and roof tiles were produced extensively. Celadon roof tiles were most ornate among roof times made with different materials, Here, the tile on the left is adorned with a peony spray encircled by a row of dots. The right-side roof tile is adorned with scrolls in relief.

Celadon with Bamboo Design in Relief,
National Treasure No. 169, Goryeo, 12th century, H. 33.6cm, Leeum, Samsung Museum of Art
This bottle is modelled after a bottle enveloped with bamboo. It has a flaring mouth, a long neck, and a bulbous body that widens towards the bottom. The neck and body are decorated in relief with bamboo, and two incised lines are used to mark the joints. The glazed surface yields a light green hue and displays crackles in parts. The mouth extends to the neck by an elegant curve, and the large lower body gives a sense of stability.

Sanghyeong Celadon

Sanghyeong (象形) celadon refers to celadon modeled after the physical shapes of figures, animals, and plants. This type of celadon simply depicts representative features of original models, giving a bold appearance. Diverse shapes of *sanghyeong* celadon include lotus flower, Korean melon, bamboo shoot, peach, lion, duck, monkey, and mythical creatures. Not overly embellished, *sanghyeong* celadon is formed elegantly and realistically, revealing the refined culture of Goryeo aristocrats without degenerating the original characteristics of Goryeo celadon.

Celadon *Girin*-shaped Incense Burner with Lid, Goryeo, 12th century, H. 20cm, Kansong Museum
This incense burner has a lid in the shape of a mythical creature *girin* (麒麟) that has the body of a deer, the tail of an ox, equine-like hoofs and mane. The *girin* sits on the lid turning its head back. Smoke comes out through the open mouth of *girin*, The lid rests on the main body which has a wide, flaring rim and three animal-shaped legs. Clouds are incised on the outer wall of the body and rim, and the brim of the lid is incised with fret pattern. The *girin*'s eyes are draws with black pigment. Overall, the burner yields a soft, jade hue.

Celadon Duck-shaped Ewer with Inlaid Design,
Treasure No. 1398, Goryeo, 12th century,
H. 15.3cm, private collection

This ewer has a globular body with a head-shaped spout and a leg-shaped handle attached on either side of the body. The back features a lotus leaf and stem. An opening is made in the center of the leaf, capped with a lotus pip-shaped lid. This is a creative piece of celadon with all its parts coordinated organically. The feathers are elaborately depicted using incising, relief, and black-and-white inlaying techniques.

Celadon Seated Arhat with Paste-on-paste White
Dot Design, National Treasure No. 173, Goryeo, 12th century, H. 22.3cm, Private Collection

This was found in Gukhwa-ri of Ganghwado Island broken into six pieces. The arhat sits on the rock-shaped pedestal with the right knee bent vertically and left knee horizontally, resting on a small table with his armed folded, and slightly lowering his head. His eyes are half shut, and he has fine eyebrows and eyes and a prominent nose. Iron-containing black pigments are applied to several places such as head, eyebrows, pupils, rock-shaped pedestal, and some folds in the garment. Using white slip, the folds are adorned with dots. The handling of the table, rock-shaped pedestal, and the figure's posture silently looking down, as if he is engaged in deep contemplation, makes this a masterpiece representing Goryeo celadon sculpture.

Celadon Tortoise-shaped Water Dropper,
Goryeo, 12th-13th century, H. 6.1cm,
National Museum of Korea

This celadon water dropper is in the shape of a dragon-headed tortoise that is often seen in *gwibu* (龜趺, tortoise-shaped pedestal) of the Goryeo Dynasty. Already during the Three Kingdoms period, Silla produced earthenware ewers in this shape. Such precedents had presumably developed into celadon versions during the Goryeo period. The mouth of the dragon head serves as an opening of the dropper. The stem of a lotus flower comes out of the mouth and extends to the back of the tortoise. The circumference of a hole for pouring water on the back of the tortoise is decorated with flower petals. The overall surface of the tortoise shell is incised with hexagonal patterns, and inside each pattern is a Chinese character "王" meaning king. The edges of the shell are sparsely adorned with pleats in half-relief. The pupils of this dragon-headed tortoise are painted with iron pigment.

Celadon with Openwork Design

Celadon with openwork (*tugak*, 透刻) design is produced by creating holes and gaps that go right through molded ceramic wares, which adds three-dimensionality and a touch of glamour. Since this decoration technique is complicated and requires refined skills, it has been used largely to adorn exclusive celadon. Only few examples decorated with openwork design, including a chair, a brush holder, a pillow, and a lid of an incense burner, remain. Moreover, as openwork design easily breaks during drying and firing, it tends to be used selectively. Celadon with openwork design is known to have been produced mainly at kilns in Gangjin and Buan during the mid-Goryeo period; however, due to the complexity of openwork technique, very few celadon wares with openwork design are extant today.

Celadon Pillow with Openwork Lotus Design, Goryeo, 12th century, H. 11.2cm,
National Museum of Korea
It resembles the pillow form of the Song Dynasty, China, but it is much more sophisticated. Except for the floor, it is overall decorated with floral and peony patterns. The peonies are done in half-relief by slanting the carving knife. The walls are decorated with a band openwork lotus scrolls, and above and below the band are scrolls done in relief. These kinds of celadon fragments have been excavated at the kiln sites in Gangjin, South Jeolla-do Province.

Celadon with Underglaze Iron Design

Celadon with underglaze iron design (*cheolhwa*, 鐵畵 or *cheolhoe*, 鐵繪) is decorated using oxidized iron pigments that turn black after being glazed and fired. Those created by applying iron-oxide pigments on their entire surface and adding glaze are called *cheolchae* (鐵彩) celadon. These celadon wares in underglaze iron belong to the category of celadon fired with reduced flames; however, many of them end up being fired with oxidized flames and having brown color. Numerous examples of celadon with underglaze iron design are adorned simply and gracefully. For instance, *Celadon Tube-shaped Bottle with Willow Design in Underglaze Iron* (National Treasure No. 113) is decorated with boldly depicted willow trees, each on its front and back sides, which adds distinctive refinement. Such artistic taste differs from that in *sanghyeong* celadon or *sanggam* (inlaid) celadon featuring delicate curves and jade-green glaze.

Celadon Bottle with Willow Design in Underglaze Iron, National Treasure No. 113, Goryeo, 12th century, H. 31.4cm, National Museum of Korea
This bottle is notable for its bold design and its composition. Although simple, the willow tree has been reinterpreted featuring a distinct, sophisticated style.

Celadon *Maebyeong* with Paste-on-paste Ginseng Leaf in Underglaze Iron, Treasure No. 340, Goryeo, 12th century, H. 27.6cm, National Museum of Korea
This *maebyeong*, or prunus vase, is painted with iron pigment, and the leaf design is carved shallow allowing white slip to fill the cavity. Then celadon glaze is applied and it is fired.

Celadon with *Sanggam* (Inlaid) Design

Celadon using *sanggam* (象嵌, inlaying) is produced by engraving motifs on the clay body, filling the carved space with white or red clay, coating the body with celadon glaze, and firing it. After fired, the carved space filled with white clay turns white, while that filled with red clay turns black. Schematic or pictorial *sanggam* designs embody the taste and sentiments of Goryeo

Celadon *Maebyeong* with Inlaid Plum Blossom, Bamboo, and Crane Design, Treasure No. 1168, Goryeo, late 12th-13th century, H. 33cm, National Museum of Korea
This is a classic example of Goryeo celadon *maebyeong*, or prunus vase, with broad shoulders and gently curved contours. Bamboo and plum trees are depicted in a lively manner on the body. The bamboo swaying in the wind leans to one side, and the plum tree stretches its two branches in opposite directions for balancing the composition. Overall, it features well- structured composition against a void background, and the images are picturesque and aristocratic.

Celadon Kundika with Inlaid Peony Design, Mid-Goryeo, H. 41.5cm, Goryeo Celadon Museum
A kundika holds pure water inside that is offered to the Buddha or Bodhitsattva in Buddhist rituals. This is made in celadon modelled after metal kundika. Peonies with leaves and stem are inlaid at regular intervals. A band of fretwork encircles the bottom end of the body. The spout was deformed during firing. A small ring attached to the tip of the spout indicates that a lid was tied to the ring. The lid is missing now.

Celadon Bowl with Inlaid Chrysanthemum Scroll Desing, National Treasure No. 115, Goryeo, 12th century, H. 6.2cm, National Museum of Korea
This bowl was found in the tomb of Mun Gong-yu, a scholar who died in 1159, together with an epitaph tablet. This is the earliest example of inlaid celadon with dates, and is important in studying the development of inlaying technique. The bowl is white inlaid with a chrysanthemum on the inner bottom and reverse inlaid with scrolls on the inner wall. The inner rim is also inlaid with a band of scrolls. There are three spur marks on the outer bottom.

people. *Celadon Prunus Vase with Inlaid Plum, Bamboo, and Crane Design* (Treasure No. 1168) evokes noble elegance in the naturalistic and relaxed depiction of cranes, particularly the one leisurely grooming its feathers. *Celadon Bowl with Inlaid Chrysanthemum Scroll Design* (National Treasure No. 115) believed to have been excavated from the tomb of Mun Gong-yu who died in 1159 serves as a significant chronicled object. The high quality of inlaid design produced around that time implies that inlaying technique began to be used even earlier.

Celadon with Paste-on-paste Design

Celadon with paste-on-paste design is executed by painting images with red or white slip using a brush. This technique is different from underglaze iron painting in that it is applied thick so as to protrude on the surface. It is usually used to add dots or lines around the incised, raised, or inlaid designs as secondary motifs.

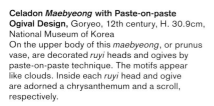

Celadon _Maebyeong_ with Paste-on-paste Ogival Design, Goryeo, 12th century, H. 30.9cm, National Museum of Korea
On the upper body of this _maebyeong_, or prunus vase, are decorated _ruyi_ heads and ogives by paste-on-paste technique. The motifs appear like clouds. Inside each _ruyi_ head and ogive are adorned a chrysanthemum and a scroll, respectively.

Celadon Gourd-shaped Ewer and Basin with Inlaid and Paste-on-paste Flowering Plant Design, Treasure No. 1930, Goryeo, 12th century, H. 29.8cm, National Museum of Korea
This is a set of ewer and basic decorated with paste-on-paste flowering plants with white and red slip. This is considered a masterpiece with bold and lively rendition of flowering plants. Black and white designs on the body maximize the contrast effect.

Celadon with Underglaze Copper Design

Celadon with underglaze copper design is decorated with copper-containing pigments that turn reddish brown after the clay body is covered with celadon glaze and fired. Painting with copper-containing pigment is called *donghwa* or *jinsa* technique, and covering copper-containing pigment to the entire surface of a vessel is called *dongchae*. According to firing conditions, copper-containing pigment turns green, black, or red. Celadon wares using *dongchae* technique exist; however, in many cases, copper pigment was restrictively used on the inlaid celadon in parts that require red hue.

Celadon Lidded Case Decorated in Underglaze Copper, Goryeo, 13th century, H. 3cm, National Museum of Korea
This is a small cylindrical case with lid. It is a rather tall container for its width, so it is could have been used as a sarira box. The upper and lower edges of the lid and the bottom edge of the body are rounded. On the top of the lid is decorated with a chrysanthemum highlighted with red copper dots. Rows of copper-red dots decorate the lid and body. This is a footless case and glazed surface yields a gray-blue hue.

Celadon Cup and Stand in Underglaze Copper, Goryeo, 12th century, H. 4.5cm, National Museum of Korea
Both the cup and stand are coated entirely with copper containing pigment. The cup is rather big for its stand. The stand has its bottom open, and it is low in form with flaring foot and cup support. These are typical features of cup and stand of the early 12th century. The copper-red is relatively vivid and soft, and red spots are found in parts. Copper pigment has volatilized around the mouth rim of the cup and also has run down the glaze displaying a celadon-like color. The bottom of the cup and stand are not applied with copper pigment and rather left in jade color.

Copper is easily volatilized when it is light in concentration and tends to smear when it is thick. It was therefore difficult to use copper pigment, and not a great number of existing celadon wares are decorated in underglaze copper. In addition to *sanggam* inlaid celadon, celadon with underglaze copper design can be regarded as another major achievement of Goryeo ceramic masters.

Celadon Gourd-shaped Ewer with Lotus Design in Underglaze Copper, National Treasure No. 133, Goryeo, 13th century, H. 33.2cm, Leeum, Samsung Museum of Art
This ewer was discovered from the tomb of Choe Hang (?-1024) and is dated to the reign of King Gojong (r. 1213-1259). It is decorated in underglaze copper around the edges of the lotus leaves which cover the entire body of the gourd-shaped ewer. The ewer is capped with a bud-shaped lid. A boy holding a lotus bud with his two hands is placed on the neck. The handle is made to resemble a scroll, and a frog sits on top of it. The spout is in the form of a rolled lotus leaf.

Celadon *Maebyeong* with Inlaid Peony Design, Treasure No. 346, Goryeo, 13th century, H. 34.5cm, National Museum of Korea
This *maebyeong*, or prunus vase, is black and white inlaid with three peonies and highlighted with copper pigment. Only a few examples of *maebyeong* are found with copper decoration. A band of fretwork encircles the foot rim, and above it is white inlaid with lotus leaves inside which is black inlaid with a grass motif. This vase features the features of 12th-century plain celadon *maebyeong*, which is divided into three sections and decorated with lotus leaves on the lower body.

Celadon with Gold-painted Design

The technique of painting in gold on the glazed surface of inlaid celadon is referred to as *geumchae, hwageum,* or *geumhwa.* Though very few in number but celadon wares painted in gold are extant today, and most of them were produced in the thirteenth century. According to *History of Goryeo* (高麗史, Goryeosa), King Chungryeol (r. 1274–1308) of Goryeo offered *onggi* (stoneware jar) painted in gold to the Yuan Dynasty in 1297. *History of Goryeo* also recorded that Jo In-gyu (1237–1308) presented celadon painted in gold as gifts to Emperor Shizu (r. 1260–1294) of the Yuan Dynasty. Existing examples of such celadon wares include *Celadon Jar with Inlaid and Gold-painted Monkey Design.* In the case of this jar found at the Goryeo palace site of Manwoldae in Kaesong, gold paint is applied on the incised lines near inlaid designs. This jar is an outstanding celadon piece in that techniques of inlaying and painting in gold are used to add glamour.

Celadon Jar with Inlaid and Gold-painted Monkey Design (fragment),
Goryeo, late 13th century, H. 25.5cm, National Museum of Korea
Unlike those of China, celadons made in Goryeo were mostly decorated in underglaze. So, only a very few extant celadon wares have been embellished with overglaze like this one, and it was done in gold. In this fragment, gold is lined around the inlaid designs. On the sides are inlaid floral scrolls which were popular at the time. This was discovered by a Japanese in around August of 1944 near a structure for drying white ginseng to the east of Manwoldae Palace site in Kaesong.

Celadon with Marbling Design

Celadon with marbling design is produced by wedging and kneading celadon clay, white clay, and kaolin with different iron contents. The mixed clay is the shaped, glazed, and fired. After fired, different types of clays kneaded turn gray, white, and black, making the glazed surface resemble the patterns found in natural marble. This type of celadon made by mixing clays with different natures is easily cracked in the production process. Nevertheless, different clay mixtures create diverse textures and patterns. Celadon wares with marbling design were produced in small quantities in the 12th century when the celadon production technology reached its peak, and very few examples are extant today. *

Celadon Cup with Marbling Design,
Goryeo, 12th century,
H. 5cm, National Museum of Korea

Learn More: Goryeo White Ware

Celadon has been thought to represent ceramics of the Goryeo Dynasty; however, white wares also began to be produced around the 10th century along with celadon wares and was made and used throughout the Goryeo period. Since the vitrification temperature of white porcelain clay is higher than that of celadon clay, Goryeo white wares were not completely vitrified. They became as hard as plaster, and the color of glaze turned ivory white tinged with light green.

Types, shapes, decoration techniques, and designs of Goryeo white wares are almost identical to those of Goryeo celadon wares. The kilns in Seo-ri, Yongin and Jungam-ri, Yeoju specialized in producing white wares. In the mid-and late Goryeo period, even Goryeo celadon kilns, such as the one in Yucheon-ri, Buan, started making decorative and refined fine-quality white wares. Representative examples of Goryeo white ware include *White Ware Maebyeong with Inlaid Peony and Willow Tree Design* and *White Ware Lidded Bowl with Inlaid Floral Medallion and Scroll Design*.

Celadon Designs

Celadon wares are decorated with various designs such as scenic views, figures, nature scenes, animals, plants, and geometrical patterns.

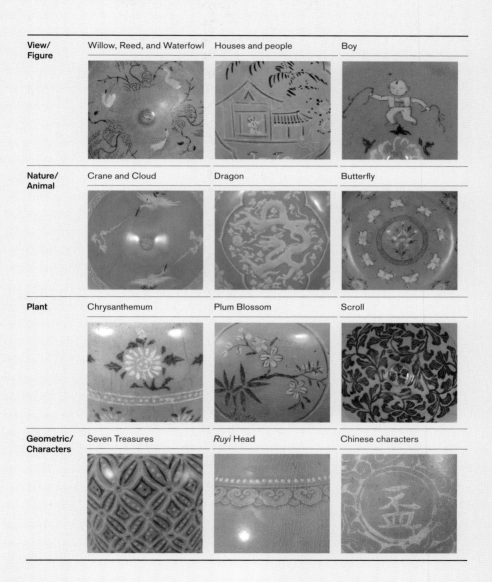

View/Figure	Willow, Reed, and Waterfowl	Houses and people	Boy
Nature/Animal	Crane and Cloud	Dragon	Butterfly
Plant	Chrysanthemum	Plum Blossom	Scroll
Geometric/Characters	Seven Treasures	*Ruyi* Head	Chinese characters

Uses of Korean Celadon

Celadon was considered not only an artwork but also a new high-tech material of everyday life. Recognition of celadon as a material resulted from the fact that celadon was used in all aspects of everyday life as bowls, roof tiles, banquet chairs, and pillows. In the following section, let us examine some practical uses of artistic celadon wares.

Tableware (Food Containers)

Imagine what kinds of food Goryeo people consumed and what types of vessels they might have used. The culinary culture that the Goryeo people enjoyed directly affected the production of Goryeo celadon. In particular, tea and wine played a significant role in creating celadon. The Goryeo people's penchant for drinking tea and wine led to the production of celadon bowls, cups, teapots, jars, bottles, and dishes in various shapes.

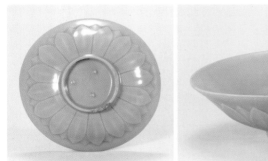

Celadon Lotus-shaped Dish in Relief, Treasure No. 1573, Goryeo, 12th century, H. 4cm, Haegang Ceramic Museum
This is an elegant and high-quality dish with an everted mouth rim, a tall and wide foot, and gently curved body. Its outer wall is decorated with lotus leaves in relief. The dish is coated with a jade-color type of glaze with a gloss. It is presumed that the dish was made at Sadang-ri kiln in Gangjin around the 12th century. There are three refractory spur marks on the outer bottom. The visual shading effect rendered by the relief designs is valuable in that it evinces the formative features of Goryeo celadon.

Celadon Spoon with Incised Dragon and Cloud Desgin, Goryeo, 12th-13th century, L. 25.5cm, National Museum of Korea

Celadon Bowl with Incised Lotus Leaves Design,
Goryeo, 12th century, H. 8.5cm, National Museum of Korea
This bowl is modelled after metal counterpart It has a square handle and is shouldered around the rim so that the lid to rest on. The incised lotus leaves are unique.

Celadon Flower-shaped Cup with Inlaid Chrysanthemum Spray Design, Mid-Goryeo, H. 7.6cm, Goryeo Celadon Museum
This cup is modelled like a flower bud with a lobed mouth rim. On the outer wall, each rib is decorated chrysanthemum, and a band of incised scrolls encircles the upper end of the cup. On the inner surface, a flower is incised on the bottom, and scrolls are incised on the wall.

Celadon Gourd-shaped Ewer, Treasure No. 1540, Goryeo, 12th century, H. 27cm, Horim Museum
This ewer features the formative characteristics of 12th-century Goryeo celadon. This ewer has a ribbed body like a melon; a spout that is shaped like a rolled-up gourd leaf; and a handle that is reminiscent of twisted gourd vines. The lid is also modelled like a gourd leaf, and the outer bottom of the ewer, which had not been carved into a foot, is also reminiscent of a gourd's base. The glaze is translucent and displays a clear and light green hue.

Writing Accoutrement

Celadon writing utensils were necessities in the studies of a Goryeo literati. A water dropper, an inkstone, a brush holder, a brush hanger, and an ink pot were found in the daily lives of the literati. These practical writing utensils in exquisite shapes and with delicate decorations embody the life and taste of Goryeo people who loved and enjoyed poetry and paintings.

Celadon Dice with Inlaid Design, Goryeo, H. 1.2cm, National Museum of Korea
This is an inlaid dice that is about 1cm in height and width. It is not exactly known where it was found. Also, other dice were recovered from the trading ship that was wrecked off the shore of Sinan on the west coast of Korea while it was sailing to Japan in the late 14th century. Dice were possibly one of play instruments that were popular during the Goryeo period.

Celadon *Girin*-shaped Water Dropper, Treasure No. 1449, Goryeo, 12th-13th century, size unknown, private collection
This water dropper is shaped after a one-horned mythical creature called girin. A tube on the back shaped like a pomegranate stem is where water is poured into and the *girin*'s mouth functions as the spout. *Girin* is holding a lotus stem in its mouth and its back is decorated with pomegranate leaves and stems. The stabilized glaze of the high celadon ear is applied thoroughly even on the foot where three spur marks are left. This is a supreme-quality piece of work done by a skillful artisan.

Celadon Duck-shaped Water Dropper,
Goryeo, 12th century, H. 7.3cm,
National Museum of Korea

Celadon Inkstone with Inlaid Inscription of "辛丑" and Chrysanthemum and Peony Design, Treasure No. 1382, Goryeo, 1181, H. 2.9cm, Leeum, Samsung Museum of Art

Celadon ink stones are barely extant, and this example is particularly significant in that it is inscribed with sexagesimal cycle and is inscribed with the names of the maker and user. The outer bottom has an white inlaid inscription that reads "辛丑五月十日造 爲大口前戶正徐散夫" and also on the side is inscribed "清沙硯壹雙黃河寺" The first two characters "辛丑" fall into years 1121, 1181, 1241, and the glaze condition and inlaid designs suggest that this was highly likely to have been produced in 1241. The two longer sides of the inkstone are black and white inlaid with peony scrolls, and the remaining two sides are inlaid with chrysanthemum scrolls and cloud designs. On the face, borders are incised with fretworks, and the inner bottom is incised with chrysanthemum sprays. The clear glaze yields a bright blue-green hue.

Celadon Monkey-shaped Seal, Goryeo, H. 3.6cm, National Museum of Korea

This is a seal with a monkey-shaped grip. Extant seals from this period are mostly made from bronze and celadon is a rare example.

Religion and Rituals

Celadon was used in Buddhist and Daoist rituals. Under the influence of Buddhism, the most dominant faith of the Goryeo Dynasty, a large quantity of celadon incense burners and kundika, which often appeared in the paintings of *Water-Moon Avalokiteshvara*, were produced. Moreover, during the Goryeo period, the burning incense became widely popular, leading to the production of various kinds of celadon incense burners in the first half of the 12th century. Large quantities of Buddhist ritual objects, including sarira containers and alms bowls, used in national ceremonies were also created.

Celadon Incense Burner with Impressed Ferocious Animal Design, Goryeo, 12th century, H. 18.4cm, National Museum of Korea
During the Goryeo Dynasty, incense burners were also created in celadon. Some of them were modeled after the form of animals and plants. However, like this incense burner, many had followed the form of *fangding*, an ancient Chinese square bowl with four legs. The body is impressed with one-legged mythical bird, *bongwhang*, and abstracted ogre faces, and legs are decorated with cicadas.

Celadon Kundika with Inlaid Mandarin Ducks and Pond Design, National Treasure No. 66, Goryeo, 12th century, H. 37cm, Kansong Museum
This kundika is white inlaid with willows, reeds, lotus, and mandarin ducks against the jade-colored background. The neck is inlaid with two peonies on the front and back. The octagonal spout stands upright on the neck. On the shoulder is attached a small mouth for pouring water into and its cap is missing.

Celadon Cup with Inlaid Inscription of "鬼", Goryeo, 13th century, H. 6.7cm, National Museum of Korea
This cup is black inlaid in four corners of the body with the character "鬼" which is encircled with white laid rings. Its function is not known, but the "鬼" inscription, meaning spirit or ghost, suggests that it could have been used in Daoist rituals.

Celadon Vessel with Inlaid Inscription of "燒錢", Goryeo, 13th century, H. 4.4cm, National Museum of Korea
This vessel is inlaid black with an inscription of "燒錢" (*sosaek*) which is part of the name of a government office responsible for holding Daoist rituals. Thus, this was likely a ritual vessel used at the office called Soseakjeon (燒錢色). A band of fretwork is incised around the mouth rim.

Celadon Dish with Inlaid Chrysanthemum Design, Goryeo, 13th century, H. 3cm, National Museum of Korea
This is a ritual vessel offered at a *Sibilyo* Daoist ritual during the Goryeo period. *Sibilyo* ritual refers to 11 planets, including the sun, moon, Mars, Mercury, Jupiter, Venus, and Saturn. During the Goryeo period, Daoist rituals were held to many constellations, including the Bid Dipper.

Furniture and Architectural Fittings

Apart from celadon dishes, Goryeo people produced a variety of celadon architectural fittings, forming part of an elegant celadon culture. They were thought to have showed an unusual interest in adorning their houses. In order to decorate their houses, Goryeo people used celadon roof tiles, celadon ornamental plaques, or celadon chairs.

In particular, celadon roof tiles were discovered not only at Gangjin kilns but also at Manwoldae (滿月臺), the royal palace in Kaesong. Diverse types of roof tiles include convex and concave roof-end tiles; flat and curved plain roof tiles; tiles at the end of roof ridge; and decorative tiles that were presumably adorned with small earthenware figurines called *japsang* (雜像).

Celadon Plaque with Inlaid Peony Design, Goryeo, 13th century, 22.6×30.6cm,
National Museum of Korea
This plaque can be divided into two ornate bands, and an ogival-shaped frame is placed inside the center which is inlaid peony sprays. The white inlaid peonies are accentuated with copper-red dots. The ogive sets against the background of densely inlaid cranes and clouds with less void space. This is a new characteristic developed at the time.

Celadon Concave Roof-tiles, Goryeo, 12th century, L. 25-26cm, National Museum of Korea

Celadon Convex Roof-end Tile with Peony Design in Relief, Goryeo, 12th century, L. 22cm, National Museum of Korea
On the round face of the tile are incised double rings. The outer register and the central roundel are respectively decorated with dots and a peony in relief.

Celadon Chair with Openwork Decoration, Goryeo, 12th century, H. 34.5cm, National Museum of Korea

Cosmetic Utensils

Although no cosmetics of the Goryeo Dynasty remain, some Goryeo celadon wares that are presumed to have been used as cosmetic containers suggest how Goryeo people may have adorned themselves. Cosmetic containers
that Goryeo females used to make themselves up include oil bottles (油瓶),
lidded bowls containing power or perfume, and a make-up box (母子盒) containing small lidded bowls and oil bottles.

Celadon Oil Bottles with Inlaid Peony Spray Design,
Goryeo, 12th century, H. 3.4cm, National Museum
of Korea
This small bottle was used to hold fragrant oil for the
hair and body. Its upper body is decorated with peony
spray designs. White-slip inlay and black-slip inlay
were applied to the flowers and leaves, respectively.
Though the designs are not realistically rendered, their
size and arrangement are in harmony with the body of
this work.

Celadon Cosmetic Box and Inner Cases with Openwork Tortoise Shell Design, Goryeo, 13th century,
H. 12.1cm, National Museum of Korea
At the time this cosmetics box was unearthed from an ancient tomb in Mosan-ri, Jangheung-gun, Jeollanam-do in
April 1939, it contained a celadon oil bottle with inlaid chrysanthemum design, a bronze mirror, and a needle case.
The shape of this box is similar to that of the lacquerware boxes used to store Buddhist scriptures. A partition in the
middle divides its interior, which is decorated with an openwork scroll design. The body and lid are decorated with
an openwork tortoise shell design.

Other Daily Items

The investigation on kiln sites in Gangjin and Buan, the centers of celadon production, indicates that a range of celadon products were created after the twelfth century when the use of celadon wares was growing and the celadon production technology reached its peak. Daily products made of celadon include oil lamps, pillows, flowerpots, and chamber pots.

Celadon Boat-shaped Chamber Pot,
Goryeo, 12th-13th century, H. 16.8cm, National Museum of Korea

Celadon Pillow with Lion Decoration,
Treasure No. 789, Goryeo, 12th century, H. 10.5cm, Leeum, Samsung Museum of Art
On a rounded rectangular base, a pair of lions—possibly male and female—sit back-to-back supporting the headrest with their heads. The lions appear lively with their eyes painted black. The headrest is in the shape of a lotus leaf. Veins of the leaf are sharply incised.

Celadon Janggo Drum with Chrysanthemum Scroll Design in Underglaze Iron, Goryeo, 14th century, H. 41.5cm, National Museum of Korea

History of Korean Celadon

Three Kingdoms and Unified Silla Periods
(Era of Northern and Southern States)

During the Three Kingdoms period, a small quantity of Chinese porcelain was excavated as tomb furnishings. By the Unified Silla period (era of Northern and Southern states), a great deal of Chinese white porcelain and celadon was circulated among the upper class and exclusively used by them. White porcelain and celadon wares imported from Tang Dynasty, China, have been discovered at the sites of large-scale temples such as Mireuksaji

Celadon Tiger-shape Chamber Pot, Later Western Qin – early Eastern Qin,
China (discovered from Baekje site) , H. 20.3cm, National Museum of Korea
This is an example of celadon tiger-shaper chamber pots that were popular in China.
The largely opened tiger's mouth functions as an opening and the tiger face attached on
the spout is rendered very realistically. An arch-shaped handle is attached from the head to
the back. Oblique lines are incised on the handle making it appear like it has been tied with
rope. Wings are also added to the body by incising. The shape and quality of the celadon
suggest that this was made in the late Western Qin or early Eastern Qin, China and was
introduced to Baekje (18 BCE-660 CE). It provides critical evidence of the exchanges that
occurred between Baekje and the Southern Dynasties of China, as well as the relationship
between the central government and local entities in Baekje.

Temple in Iksan and Hwangryongsaji Temple in Gyeongju as well as at the historical site of Cheonghaejin on the Jangdo Island in Wando-gun. This implies that Korea had been interested in porcelains since early days and that the steadily increasing demand for Chinese porcelain led to the production of porcelain in Korea.

Korea began producing celadon in the Goryeo period on the basis of the high-fired earthenware tradition of Unified Silla and under the influence of China. Scholars have presented different views on when exactly celadon started to be made. Recent excavation surveys revealed that ceramic masters of Yuezhouyao kiln in Zhejiang Province, China, might have begun the production of celadon mainly to make tea bowls.

Celadon Jar, Eastern Qin, China (discovered from Baekje site), H. 37.6cm, National Museum of Korea
In 1969, large quantities of earthenware and metalwork were discovers in Baekje tombs. This jar has a dish-shaped mouth, a short neck, a wide-shouldered body, and a flat foot. Two small jugs are attached on the shoulders, and above them are brown decorations. The jar is covered overall with brownish celadon glaze, but parts of the lower body and base are unglazed. Similar Chinese counterparts were found in Xiangshan Tomb No. 5 (Tomb of Wang Zhong, CE 358), Tomb No. 3 (Tomb of Wang Dan Hu, CE 359), and Tomb of Wang Xing's Couple (CE 341, 348) in Nanjing, as well as in Dongying Xingning No. 2 Tomb (CE 364)in Hangzhou. Most of them were Eastern Qin celadon wares of Yue kiln dated to the 4th century. Therefore this jar, discovered in Hwaseong-ri, was possibly imported to Baekje through trading with the Southern Dynasties, China, and was introduced to local entities in the regions of Hwaseong-ri.

Birth of Goryeo Celadon

The kiln sites of early celadon indicate two traditions of celadon production. Celadon and white wares were fired in large-scale brick-built kilns located in the mid-west regions including Gyeonggi-do on the Korean Peninsula, while small mud-built kilns centered in the southwestern regions such as Gangjin were used to produce celadon and black wares. Goryeo celadon wares in its early stage were created using the celadon production technology and the kiln operation methods that were modeled after those of China. A considerable number of early Goryeo celadon resembled Chinese celadon.

The early celadon kilns in the midwest and southwestern regions of Korean Peninsula show differences in structure and final product, which is characteristic of early Goryeo celadon production. In the midwest areas such as Baecheon, Hwanghae-do and Siheung and Yongin, Gyeonggi-do, 40-meter-long large-scale brick-built kilns (*jeonchuk-yo*, 塼築窯) influenced

Celadon Bowl with Inscription of "癸丑年造上大聖持鉢", Goryeo, 12th century, H. 8.3cm, National Museum of Korea
This is a thin-walled bowl is in the form of a Buddhist alms bowl with an upright mouth and a low foot. It is glazed in light brown. Glaze has been wiped off from the foot ring and coarse grains of sand were used as kiln spurs. In two rows, an inscription of "癸丑年造上大聖持鉢" is black inlaid on the outer surface. It is believed to have been made in 1073.

by Yuezhou kilns were constructed. In those kilns, white porcelain as well as celadon resembling Yuezhou ware were produced using diverse types of saggars (*gapbal*, 匣鉢). On the other hand, in the southwestern regions including Gangjin, South Jeolla-do, 20-meter-long small mud-built kilns (*tochuk-yo*, 土築窯) were built. In such kilns, Yuezhou-style celadon and Korean-style black ware were produced using simpler saggars.

Celadon Flower Vase with Inscription of "青林寺",
Goryeo, 10th-11th century, H. 12.1cm,
National Museum of Korea
This is a rare form of Goryeo celadon flower vase. On the front and back of the body are written in underglaze iron "青林寺" "天堂花○", respectively. It is still not known what the inscriptions mean. However, "寺" (temple) and "花" (temple) suggest that it could have been a flower vase used in Buddhist temples. Dark green glaze is applied thick and opaque with lots of air bubbles.

Celadon Ewer, Treasure No. 1453, Goryeo,
H. 21.3cm, Horim Museum
This is modelled after Goryeo bronze ewer. The glaze, clay body, spurs on the foot of this ewer represent special features of early Goryeo celadon. There are other similar examples of the period but this one is skillfully made and in good shape.

Proliferation of Celadon Culture and Completion of Jade-colored Glaze

In the 11th century, high-quality celadon was produced mainly in the Gangjin and Buan districts. In order to satisfy local demand, kilns were operated in other areas such as Gyeongseo-dong in Incheon and Jinan-san in Incheon, producing a so-called "green celadon". During this period, production technology became more sophisticated than in the early days, but celadon was still under the influence of China. Celadons were decorated with diverse techniques and were categorized accordingly. While there were also plain celadon, most were adorned by incising, carving, impressing, paining in underglaze iron, and applying paste on paste.

Goryeo celadon has developed remarkably since the middle of the 11th century and has reached the peak with highly sophisticated noble wares from the 12th century. During the reign of King Yejong (r. 1105-1122) Chinese elements almost disappeared in Goryeo celadon, and during the reigns of King Injong and Uijong unique Goryeo celadon wares were produced. Since then, Goryeo celadon was referred to as celadon of jade color, or *bisaek*. In his *Xuanhe fengshi Gaoli tujing*, a travelogue of the Song China envoy, Xu Jing (徐兢) said "the Goryeo people refer to the blue or green of their ceramics as "*bisaek*." In recent years, these pieces have been made with great skill, and the luster has become especially fine." This shows that Goryeo people call the color of celadon *bisaek* (翡色, "jade color") , which differed

Celadon Cup with Scroll Design in Underglaze Iron, Goryeo, 11th century, H. 6.1cm, National Museum of Korea
Celadon wares discovered in 1983 from the seas off Yaksan-myeon, Wando-gun, in South Jeolla-do Province included some celadon vessels decorated in underglaze iron. They are believed to have been produced in Jinsa-ri kilns in Haenam-gun, South Jeolla-do Province. It has a wide mouth and a small foot and is decorated with scrolls on the back and front. Gray-blue celadon glaze is applied, and three refractory clay marks are on the foot where glaze has been wiped off.

from the *bisaek* (秘色, "secret color"). The people of Goryeo were proud of their jade-colored celadon. Chinese elites highly appraised the jade color of Goryeo celadon , and this is shown in *Brocade on the Sleeve*, a book written by a Chinese connoisseur whose sobriquet is Taiping Laoren. In the book, he stated that Chinese Ding ware and Goryeo celadon of jade-colored glaze were the first under heaven.

Celadon Square Stand, Goryeo, 12th century,
H. 8.6cm, National Museum of Korea
This stand has been known to be discovered in the tomb of King Injong (r. 1122-1146) in Jangdan-gun, Gyeonggi-do Province. Also, believed to have made a set with another identical piece, this stand was possibly used to hold confectionery in rituals. Fragments of same shape and quality were found in the Sadang-ri kiln sites in Gangjin, South Jeolla-do Province. A small square stand of the same shape made in Yue kiln, Song, China is also housed in Ashmolean Museum in Oxford, UK. A gray-green glaze is applied with a high gloss and crackles are rarely found. This stand is made with great skill representing the early-12th century celadon which was during the prime of plain celadon.

Celadon Lidded *Maebyeong* with Incised Lotus Design, National Treasure No. 254, Goryeo, 12th century, H. 43cm, Private Collection
This is the only surviving *maebyeong*, or prunus vase, with its lid remaining. With its dignified form and sophisticated designs, this unique *maebyeong* represents the early-12th century celadon. In the classic form of the mid-Goryeo period, it is proportioned most ideally with a rather wide mouth, swollen shoulders and a slender bottom. In four parts of the body, lotus leaves are incised in fine lines.

Inlaid Celadon and the Popularization of Diverse Decoration Methods

Goryeo celadon was decorated beautifully and in a sophisticated way using different techniques: relief, incising, openwork, modeling physical shapes (*sanghyeong*), inlaying, underglaze iron, underglaze copper, and paste-on-paste. Types of celadon ware range from daily products to architectural fittings such as roof tiles. The most remarkable achievements of Goryeo celadon were the completion of jade-green celadon with the subdued sheen and the development of *sanggam* technique that breaks new ground in ceramic art.

During its golden age of the mid-twelfth century, Goryeo *sanggam* celadon was splendid in its presentation of refined inlaid design and restrained yet elegant form; however, since the end of the twelfth century, it had lost its charm. Furthermore, jade-green glaze had faded, had lost luster, and had become opaque.

Celadon Bottle-shaped Ewer with Inlaid Crane, Cloud, and Chrysanthemum Design, Treasure No. 1451, Goryeo, 12th century, Horim Museum Made with great skill, this ewer boasts a fine shape, inlaid design, and a glaze color. The inlaid patterns are organically displayed and structured. A chrysanthemum is encircled by a dual ring and between the ringed chrysanthemums are cranes. Black and white inlaying clay have well fused with the clay body where the inlaid designs are flat, and the colors of inlaid patterns are also uniformed. It is glazed rather thickly but evenly, and the glaze is clear and lustrous. The ewer is ornate and elegant.

The Demise of Celadon and Celadon Inscribed with the Sexagenary Cycle

In the thirteenth century, the long war with Yuan Dynasty, China impoverished Goryeo's economy, thus leading to the decline in quality of Goryeo celadon. Crude and simple forms replaced elegant curves; the thickness of bowls increased; the glaze color turned dark greenish brown or yellowish brown. Celadon with inlaid inscription newly emerged.

Some of them were inscribed with the sexagenary cycle (*ganji*, 干支) and were called *ganjimyeong* celadon. Extant examples of *ganjimyeong* celadon are inscribed with "gisa" (己巳), "gyeongo" (庚午), "imsin" (壬申), "gyeyu" (癸酉), "gapsul" (甲戌), "imo" (壬午), "jeonghae" (丁亥), and "eulmi" (乙未) among the sixty terms of the sexagenary cycle. The emergence of *ganjimyeong* celadon in the late-Goryeo period presumably resulted from the intention to enhance the quality of celadon that had been lowered due to the lengthy war

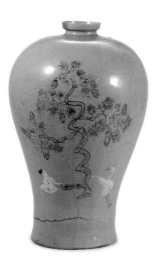

Celadon *Maebyeong* with Inlaid Design of an Old Man Playing the Musical Instrument, Goryeo, late 12th-13th century, H. 30.9cm, National Museum of Korea
This vase is decorated with small and large pine trees. and around the trees are an old man playing the *geomungo*, a crane, and a boy. The old man's face and posture, the pine tree, and the dancing crane are depicted naturally.

Celadon Bowl with Inlaid Flower and Insect Design, Goreyo, 13th century, H. 8.3cm, National Museum of Korea
Nameless flowers and insects were used to decorate the 13th-century Goryeo celadon. On the inner wall are inlaid flower sprays and insects, and the outer surface is reverse inlaid with four chrysanthemums against the background of reverse inlaid scrolls.

with Mongols and to prevent the exploitation of celadon, the major tribute of Goryeo. Surviving wares include bowls, dishes, four-eared jars, cups, stem cups and are decorated with inlaid designs of flowers and insects, waterfront landscape, lychee, crane and cloud, chrysanthemum, phoenix and cloud, and lotus flowers and scrolls, which were popular in the late Goryeo period. The quality of these wares was relatively better than that of other celadon wares created in the same period. However, compared to celadon wares from the mid Goryeo period, they were inferior in quality as they came to have thicker walls and cruder shapes. This qualitative decline accelerated in the fourteenth century.

The qualitative depreciation of celadon was closely related to Goryeo's social and economic issues, such as external confusion that Goryeo faced during the Yuan intervention period and the corruption of Goryeo aristocrats. In the late-fourteenth century, the appearance of Japanese raiders

Celadon jar with Inlaid Dragon and Cloud Design, Goryeo, 13th century, H. 25cm, National Museum of Korea
This is one of the finest examples of late-Goryeo celadon inlaid jars with an elegant form and designs. The white inlaid designs protrude, and the dragons on the front and back are particularly embossed. A similar piece of fragment was found in Yucheon-ri kiln sites in Buan-gun, South Jeolla-do Province.

Celadon Bowl with Inlaid Inscription of "己巳" **and Lotus Scroll Design,** Goryeo, 14th century, H. 8.2cm, National Museum of Korea
This late Goryeo celadon bow is inscribed with "己巳", a sexagesimal cycle. A schematized design of lotus scrolls decorates the inner surface, and simple, white inlaid scrolls adorn the outer wall. Lower body is stamped and inlaid with lotus leaves

devastated the southern areas of the Korean Peninsula. Accordingly, ceramic masters of Gangjin, the principle manufacturing place of celadon, fled inland, resulting in the spread of celadon kilns throughout the country. The poor production circumstances lowered the quality of celadon, but brought about an unexpected result of broadening the class of its users. The deteriorated style of the late Goryeo sanggam celadon continued during the Joseon period, serving as the prototype of *buncheong* (粉靑沙器) ware.

Celadon Bottle with Inlaid Lotus Scroll and Dragon Design in Underglaze Copper, Treasure No. 1022, Goryeo, 14th century, H. 38.3cm, Horim Museum
This bottle is densely decorated accentuated with underglaze copper design. A gray-green glaze is thinly covered but not in a good condition. Parts of the upper body have oxidized yielding a light brown hue. Six bands of design encircle the neck. The first three are inlaid with fretwork and lotus designs, and below them are black inlaid with lotus, chrysanthemum, and crane and cloud. The shoulders are white inlaid with flowers inside that are dotted in underglaze copper. Inside the four large circles on the body are inlaid a dragon holding in its mouth a copper-red jewel.

Celadon *Maebyeong* with Inlaid Lotus and Willow Design and Inscription of "德泉", Treasure No. 1452, Goryeo, 14th century, H. 27.8, Horim Museum
Of all celadon wares inscribed with "德泉", this is the finest and rarest example with its form, design, and glaze in a good condition. A band of *ruyi* heads decorates the shoulders and below it are lotus flowers. The body is inlaid with schematized waves above which are inlaid lotus flowers and willows. This is a transitional celadon example between the Goryeo celadon and *buncheong* ware.

Joseon Dynasty

The two leading ceramic wares of the Joseon Dynasty were *buncheong* ware carrying the tradition of Goryeo celadon and white porcelain produced using the new technology imported from Ming Dynasty, China. Besides, a very small amount of celadon was produced in white porcelain kilns. Until the mid-seventeenth century, celadon continued to be made at white porcelain official kilns in Gwangju, Gyeonggi-do that exclusively produced ceramic wares used by the royal family and officials.

Celadon of the Joseon Dynasty was made from white clay rather than gray clay often used in Goryeo celadon and coated with blue glaze. Shapes of Joseon celadon are largely similar to those of white porcelain, and decoration methods of Joseon celadon owe much to the famed celadon tradition of the preceding Goryeo Dynasty. Various records document that celadon wares were used at the Palace of the Crown Prince (Donggungjeon). This shows that Joseon court following the strict social hierarchy of Confucianism used celadon as the vessels of the Crown Prince in order to distinguish them from white porcelain tableware. Considering that only a few Joseon celadon wares remain intact, not many celadon wares were produced during the Joseon period.

Celadon Bowl with Cloud Design in Relief, Joseon, 15th century, H. 7.9cm, National Museum of Korea
This bowl is coated with celadon glaze over white porcelain clay body. The bowl is in the classic form of the 15th century white ware and *buncheong* bowl.

Celadon Lidded Jar, Treasure No. 1071, Joseon, 15th century, H. 23.4cm (overall), Horim Museum
This jar with lid is in the shape of early-Joseon white porcelain jar. The jar has its mouth rolled out for reinforcement. The swollen shoulders are tempered toward the bottom. The jar is rather wide for its height. The lid is tiered and has a flower-bud-shaped knob. It is built with white porcelain clay and a light green celadon glaze applied overall with stains in parts. This type of jar was made in small quantities for the court's use.

The Production and Circulation (Transportation) of Celadon

During the Goryeo period, supplies used by the royal family and central offices were paid for through taxes collected from local regions based on prefecture and county administrative system. Ceramics, ink, and paper were produced in special administrative districts called *hyang*, *so*, and *bugok*, which were particularly responsible for producing ceramics. The most representative *so* was the one in Daegu (present-day Daegu-hyeon) located in Gangjin, Jeollanam-do. The kilns located near Gaegyeong (present-day Gaeseong), the capital of Goryeo, in the initial stage of celadon production were moved to the Jeolla-do regions in the eleventh century. Afterwards, Gangjin and Buan became major manufacturing places, offering ceramic wares to the royal family and central government officials. Since Gangjin and Buan were distant from Gaegyeong, the principal place of ceramic consumption, there must have been difficulties in transporting fragile ceramics.

Such challenges were overcome by the marine transportation system (*joun*, 漕運) completed in the eleventh year of the reign of King Seongjong (成宗, r. 981–997). Celadon wares produced in the regions distant from

Celadon Toad-shaped Ink Stone with Paste-on-paste Design, Treasure No. 1782, Goryeo, 12th century, H. 7cm, National Research Institute of Maritime Cultural Heritage
This was discovered in the waters off the Dae Island of Geunheung-myeon, Taean-gun, South Chungcheong-do Province along with bowls, dishes, ewers, incense burners, and wooden tags, among others. The wooden tag with the ink inscription of "耽津縣在京隊正仁守戶付沙器壹" shows that ship was carrying ceramics made in Gangjin to an official named In Su in Gaegyeong.
This is the only remaining inkstone made in the shape of a toad. With its four legs folded, the crouching toad appears to be looking for a prey. Toad's skin has been depicted with underglaze iron-red dots and white paste. The grinding area is made flat yet tilted on the back of the toad and it is left unglazed. Rows of semi-circles have been incised densely so that inkstick can be efficiently ground. This is significant in that its production date and place and supplier and user have been identified.

Gaegyeong came to be transported rather easily by ships. Goryeo celadon comprises the largest portion of the artifacts that have been continuously excavated from the recently discovered shipwrecks on the west coast of the Korean peninsula. Many ships that departed *jochang* (漕倉, warehouses to store regional products and grain) on the west coastal route were shipwrecked due to dangerous sea currents and bad weather conditions, while heading for Gaegyeong. These shipwrecks have been found in the west coastal areas, such as Eoduri village in Wando, Wonsando Island in Boryeong, Doripo in Muan, Yamido Island in Gunsan, Biando Island, Munyeodo Island, Sipyidongpado Island, Daeseom Island in Taean, and Mado Island. From now on, important evidences that will shed light on the production and circulation of Goryeo celadon are expected to be found through underwater excavations.

Celadon *Maebyeong* with Inlaid Chrysanthemum, Peony, Willow and Reed Design / Wooden Tag, Goryeo, late 12th-early 13th century, *Maebyeong*: H. 39.1cm, Tag: L. 13.4cm, National Research Institute of Maritime Cultural Heritage
Both relics have been discovered in the seas off Mado Island in Geunheung-meyong, Taean-gun, South Chungcheong-do Province. The ribbed jar is vertically divided into six sections and each section is inlaid with chrysanthemum, peony, willow, reed, and bamboo, respectively. The vase was found with a wooden tag, on which is written "重房都將校吳文富" on the front "宅上眞盛樽封" on the back. The inscription reads that sesame oil bottled in a *jun* jar is sent to O Mun-bu, a military official of Council of Generals. This also reveals that this type of vase was called "*jun*" at the time, and sesame oil was stored in a *maebyeong*, or pronus vase. This is an important material for studying the function, usage, designation, production date, user of the *maebyeong* as well as the social aspects of the time.

Chapter 2

Materials
and Tools
for Making
Celadon

Clay, the Materials of Celadon

Raw materials for making celadon include clay ($Al_2O_3 \cdot 2SiO_2 \cdot 2H_2O$), silica ($SiO_2$), and feldspar ($KNaO \cdot Al_2O_3 \cdot 6SiO_2$), which are produced from natural sources. Clay is naturally sedimentary clay containing 2-3% iron, and it is an essential raw material that can build and maintain the shape of celadon. Silica acts as a structure so that the shape of the celadon does not change even when it is fired, and feldspar is a molten raw material that imparts rigid properties during the firing process.

Materials and Clay of Celadon

Clay   White Clay (Kaolin)   Pottery Stone

Clay body

Celadon clay is made by mixing clay, silica and feldspar for plasticity and vitrification. In the Goryeo period, celadon clay was made from clay, silica and feldspar minerals, and celadon was made with a similar clay regardless of the area and time of production. Goryeo celadon shows a change in celadon color depending on the content of iron contained in the clay, and may be classified into high-grade celadon and low-grade celadon depending on the coarseness of the particles constituting the clay.

Clay Bodies of Goryeo Celadon

 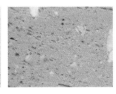 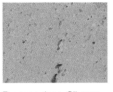 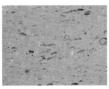

| Sadang-ri, Gangjin | Sindeok-ri, Haenam | Bangsan-dong, Siheung | Seo-ri, Yongin |

Structures of Goryeo Celadon Clay Body (scanning electron microscope images, 100 magnifications)

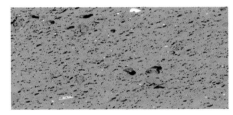 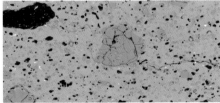

Samheung-ri, Gangjin   Sindeok-ri, Haenam

Chemical Composition of Goryeo Celadon from the Kiln Sites
Source: Kang Gyeong-in, "Kiln Structures of Goryeo Celadon and Changes in Color",
Characteristics of Colors in Goryeo Celadon, Gangjin Celadon Museum, 2010.

	SiO_2	Al_2O_3	Fe_2O_3	MgO	CaO	Na_2O	K_2O	TiO_2	P_2O_5	MnO
Seo-ri, Yongin	73.90	17.44	2.70	0.92	0.38	1.06	2.61	0.94	0.02	0.02
Bangsan-dong, Siheung	75.82	15.85	1.97	0.74	0.59	0.94	3.16	0.68	0.03	0.03
Samheung-ri, Gangjin	73.25	19.64	2.69	0.65	0.32	0.30	2.19	0.93	0.02	0.01
Sindeok-ri, Haenam	75.60	17.10	2.45	0.23	0.70	0.66	2.39	0.85	0.02	0.02

Pigments Used in Celadon

Pigments used for decorating and coloring celadon contain iron and copper, using natural minerals or metal such as copper depending on iron content. Representative natural minerals used as pigments are white and red clays used in inlay technique. Pigments made of clay, red clay, etc. containing iron are used for decoration techniques in underglaze iron-brown pigment and painting. Pigments used for decoration in underglaze copper are made by mixing about 1% of copper oxide with natural minerals that hardly contain any iron. Such pigments are referred to as high-temperature pigments or inorganic pigments, depending on their ability to develop without being volatilized at high temperatures.

Inlaying

This technique of decoration involves etching the desired motifs on the leather-hard clay body and filling in the cavities with white or red slip. Depending on the color of the slips displayed after they are fired, they are called white inlaying slip and black inlaying slip. White clay containing less than 0.5% iron is used to make white slip, and red clay containing about 8% iron is used for black inlaying slip.

Underglaze Copper

Underglaze copper decoration involves painting on bisque-fired wares with copper pigment or covering the entire vessel with it. Vessels decorated with the cooper pigment are glazed and then fired in a reduction atmosphere, and the copper decoration displays a red hue. Copper oxide and copper carbonate are used mainly for underglaze copper decoration, and they yield a red color when fired in a reduction atmosphere and a green hue by oxidation firing. Copper is difficult to handle as it tends to volatilize or smear during firing.

Materials, Slips, and Motifs for Inlaying

White Clay   White Slip   White Inlaid Design

Red Clay   Black Slip   Black Inlaid Design

Copper Oxide for Underglaze Copper Decoration, Copper Pigment, Copper Decoration

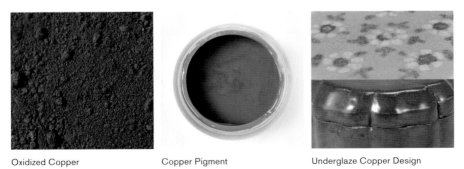

Oxidized Copper   Copper Pigment   Underglaze Copper Design

Glaze of Celadon

Celadon glaze is one of the determinants of the color of celadon. It is classified as limestone glaze based on the type of raw material which plays an important role in fusing. The celadon glaze in the limestone glaze type has been used for a long time for Goryeo celadon, and it is still used for producing modern celadon wares. The raw materials of celadon glaze include white clay, clam shells, and ashes of plants. White clay refers to pottery stone that is used as material for glaze including silica, feldspar, and clay minerals. In general, limestone and ash are important raw materials in celadon glaze that are used as solvents. What is notable is that in the Gangjin areas clam shells are used in making celadon glaze.

Raw Materials for Celadon Glaze and Glaze of the Gangjin Region

White Clay   Clam Shells   Ash

Glaze

The glaze of Goryeo celadon is a limestone glaze type containing 13-20% calcium oxide, but its content differed depending on production area and time. The content of phosphorus oxide (P_2O_5) contained in glaze reveals that plant ash has been used rather than limestone as a source of calcium oxide to make the glaze of Goryeo celadon. In general, the color of Goryeo celadon is the color developed by the chemical reaction caused by the reduction firing of the clay body and iron oxide in the glaze. In fact, it has been observed that Goryeo celadon displays various colors ranging from green-blue to brownish green. The iron content of the celadon glaze is about 2%; however, the color change of celadon glaze is more dependent on oxidation or reduction in the kiln atmosphere rather than the content of iron. Fine bubbles are observed in the thick glaze layer of Goryeo celadon. The color of Goryeo celadon changes due to absorption, scattering, and reflection by these bubbles.

Glaze Layer of Goryeo Celadon

   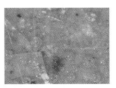

| Sadang-ri, Gangjin | Sindeok-ri, Haenam | Seo-ri, Yongin | Bubbles in glaze |

Chemical Components of Goryeo Celadon Glaze (%)
Source: Kang Gyeong-in, "Kiln Structures of Goryeo Celadon and Changes in Color",
Characteristics of Colors in Goryeo Celadon, Gangjin Celadon Museum, 2010.

	SiO_2	Al_2O_3	Fe_2O_3	MgO	CaO	Na_2O	K_2O	TiO_2	P_2O_5	MnO
Stratum 1 of Jungdeok, Seo-ri, Yongin	57.32	13.69	2.37	3.57	15.24	2.51	1.75	0.97	1.62	0.95
Stratum 2 of Jungdeok, Seo-ri, Yongin	61.40	14.62	2.39	3.83	9.77	2.31	2.44	0.79	1.66	0.80
Bangsan-dong, Siheung	59.50	13.56	2.17	1.48	16.95	1.59	1.80	0.93	1.26	0.65
Samheung-ri, Gangjin	58.92	13.20	2.61	1.37	14.35	2.31	2.54	0.92	2.33	1.45
Sindeok-ri, Haenam	55.35	12.97	2.04	3.07	20.69	1.58	2.05	1.04	0.52	0.69

Facilities and Equipment of Workshop

The workshop is furnished with various facilities and tools for producing celadon. There are facilities and tools necessary for storing and processing of raw materials, as well as for the process of shaping vessels before firing them. In the past, celadon kilns were equipped with different facilities and tools nearby, and potters divided their works according to the process of making celadon. Nowadays, workshops that make clay and glaze of celadon are separated from the workshops that shape and fire them.

Facilities for Processing Raw Materials and Tools

Material Storage

Clay minerals used as main raw materials in making celadon are collected in large quantities and stored in outdoor storage facilities. (See figure on p.84) While kept in outdoor storage for a long period of time, the quality of

(Indoor) Material Storage

the clay becomes more appropriate for shaping ceramics. The grains of clay become finer and its viscosity increases as it ages by repeated freezing, defrosting, and weathering processes. Other materials such as kaolin, pottery stone, and red clay are kept in indoor storage facilities to prevent them from mixing with other raw materials or impurities.

Ball Mill

A ball mill is the most commonly used machine for grinding raw materials for producing celadon. The ball mill consists of a hollow cylindrical shell rotating and ball-shaped grinding media inside it. The cylindrical shell is made of metal, but the inner walls are made of hard rock to prevent mixing of iron. There are balls inside the cylinder, and to grind materials more efficiently the balls are of various sizes. When the raw materials and water are put inside and rotated, the raw material is fractioned and crushed between the inner wall of the mill and the balls.

The ball mill is used in place of the traditional levigation process or used as a raw material processing tool for the purpose of crushing the solid minerals. On the other hand, the mill is also used for producing glazes or making trial glazes. In this case, small mills made of ceramics are used.

Ball Mill

Levigation Facility

This is a traditional facility for removing impurities such as sand grains from raw materials of celadon to obtain high purity materials. As for the levigation facility in the Joseon Dynasty, there was a tank shaped like a pit in the ground with a diameter of 1-2 meters and a depth of 1 meter.

In the present day, levigation facilities are also used in processing raw materials and making clay. For such purposes, the facility is equipped with rectangular-shaped cement tank as well as other different mechanical facilities. Mechanical equipment includes agitators for making slip by mixing water and raw materials; electric vibrating strainer for sifting different sizes of particles; and electromagnetic de-ironing devices capable of removing metal dust; and filter press that removes a certain amount of water from clay slip, etc. Furthermore, it is possible to process raw materials, including levigation, and to manufacture clay. Rectangular cement tanks function not only as levigation tanks in the traditional way, but also as storage tanks for clay or slip that have finished the sieving and de-ironing process or mixing different clays and slips.

Rectangular Cement Tanks at Levigation Facilities

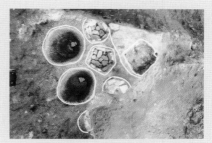
Sieve

A sieve is a tool to filter grains and sand grains roughly and finely. In ceramic making, it is a tool that is used to filter slip or glaze as a levigation. Traditionally sieves are made of fibrous materials such as hemp, but they are also made of metals such as copper that do not rust. The size of the sieve hole is expressed as a mesh, and the unit *mok* is used in Korea.

Sieve

Pug Mill

This is a machine that kneads clay suitable for shaping ceramic vessels. A vacuum pug mill is most widely used among potters, and it has a vacuum pump added to remove fine bubbles from clay. By using the vacuum pug mill, it is possible to prevent defects such as abnormal shrinkage, cracks and bubble expansion that may occur during drying or firing.

Pug Mill

Facilities and Tools at a Workshop

Potter's Wheel

A potter's wheel is a tool that uses rotational motion for shaping ceramics. There are different types: hand wheel span by hand; kick wheel spun by kicking with foot; electric wheel generated by electricity. Traditionally, kick wheel was used most widely, but nowadays, it is used only when building large *onggi*. Generally, the electric wheel is the most commonly used because it is easy to adjust the speed while spinning.

Electric Wheel

Mulgajuk

Mulgajuk, meaning "water leather," is used to finish the mouth of a vessel. It is soaked in water before use.

Mulgajuk

JJaeljul or Cutting Wires

JJaeljul, also called *samjul* and *seonro*, is made of wire, thread, or fishing line. It has a handle on one or both ends. It is a tool used to cut the bottom end of a vessel after the vessel has been shaped on the wheel.

JJaeljul or Cutting Wires

Gupkal

This tool is bent at its tip and is used to trim the foot and smooth out the surface by scraping.

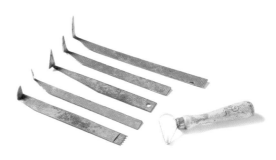

Gupkal

Chucks or *Guptong*

Gooptong, or a chuck, is used when trimming the foot or finishing the shape of vessels. Depending on the kinds of vessel, a variety of shapes were used. Chucks are made together with vessels with the same clay, which ensured a similar level of dryness between the vessels and the chuck.

Chucks or *Guptong*

Boards

Boards are used to both dry and transport the thrown vessels. They are made of pine or plywood. Depending on the condition of the drying room and other facilities various sizes of boards are used.

Boards

Graving Knives

These knives are used to apply designs on ceramics by incising or carving. Sometimes they are made by potters themselves with metal such as umbrella ribs.

Graving Knives

Inlaying Knives

These knives are used for filling in the cavities with clay and scraping off the residues from the surface. They are made by grinding metal plates

Inlaying Knives

Stamps

These stamps used to apply motifs on the ceramic surface. They are made with the clay to press designs and they are hardened by first firing.

Stamps

Kilns and Firing Equipment

Kiln

The kiln is an essential facility for making ceramic wares. Depending on the draft of the flame, kilns can largely be categorized into downdraft kiln, updraft kiln, and crossdraft kiln. Also, there are wooden, oil, gas, and electric kilns depending on the fuel that is fed into it.

Climbing Kiln

A climbing kiln, or tunnel kiln, is built on a slope from the stoke hole to the firing chambers through which flames draft up to the flue. This is a traditional, updraft kiln fueled with wood. It consists of a stoke hole, firing chambers where vessels are stacked, and a flue through which smoke escapes. To the right or left side of each chamber there is a a doorway to facilitate inserting and stacking vessels, and also to take them out.

Traditional kiln (climbing kiln)

Gas Kiln

Gas kilns using gas as a fuel mainly use LPG, but some use LNG. Regardless of the type of gas, the kiln is made in a similar format. Inside the box-shaped iron structure, there is a wall built of insulating bricks and refractory bricks, and there is a kiln door that can be opened and closed in the front. The interior ceiling of the kiln is made elliptical using trapezoidal bricks without iron structures so that it can ensure the efficient flow of flame and be stable even with gas explosion. A torch is installed in the hole located at the lower left and right of the kiln, and the temperature is raised by burning the gas.

In the gas kiln, the flames gather up from the torch on the left and right sides of the kiln to the central part of the ceiling, and then escapes to the flue through the bottom of the kiln. Such downdraft structure allows less variation in temperature at the top, bottom, left and right sides of the kiln. A damper can be installed in the middle of the flue to facilitate the fire control of oxidation and reduction atmosphere inside the kiln.

Gas Kiln

Electric Kiln

An electric kiln using electricity as a heat source is comprised of refractory bricks and metal heating elements inside the kiln, and a controller on the outside for regulating the amount of electricity according to the temperature. The heating element, which is an important part of the electric kiln, varies in calorific value and price depending on the kind of heating element. It is possible to set the temperature and time via the controller to fire the vessels in a very convenient and stable temperature. The electric kiln is not a fuel combustion type, so it is impossible to carry out the fire control of oxidation and reduction. In order to solve such disadvantage of the electric kiln, there is an electric kiln that uses either a reducing agent or the gas control device.

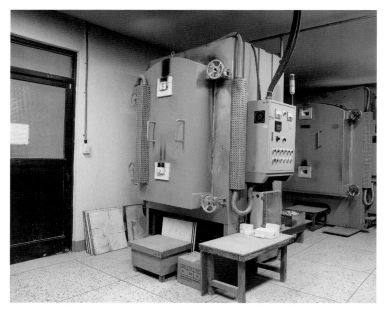

Electric Kiln

During the Goryeo Dynasty, the climbing kiln was built at an angle of about 10-12°, so that the flow of flames would continue from the stoking hole to the flue through the firing chambers where the celadon wares are fired. The climbing kilns for Goryeo celadon are divided into a brick-built kiln and a mud-built kiln, depending on how they are made. Brick-built kilns generally have a width of about 2m and are about 40m long. Mud-built kiln are about 10m long, when small, and large ones are about 20m long. Both types are 1.2-1.4m in width. Brick-built kilns were used the most in the mid-west region (Gyeonggi Province) and mud-built kilns in the southwestern region (Jeolla province), and there was a difference in kiln operation depending on the kiln's construction method, scale, and area.

 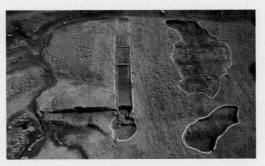

Brick-built kiln (Bangsan-dong, Siheung, Gyeonggi-do Province)

Mud-built kiln (Sadang-ri no 43, Sadang-ri, Gangjin, Jeolla-do Province)

Firing Tools

Firewood

In traditional kilns, wood is used to fire ceramics and pine was mostly used. For efficient combustion, the pine tree is divided into a certain size and prepared as firewood. When using a traditional kiln, firewood worth 10 times the weight of the vessels is needed.

Firewood

Saggar

A saggar is a container used to encase ceramic ware when using the climbing kiln. A saggar prevents the vessels from being discolored by wood ash. It ensures a fine quality of ceramic ware by blocking off flames and radiant heat.

Saggar

Shelves and Posts

These are the tools used in stacking vessels inside the kiln. Vessels are placed on these refractory plates or shelves made of silicon carbide that is black and high in fire resistance. During the firing, a white alumina is applied on the top of the fire plate to prevent it from adhering to the vessels. The kiln posts made of mullite with high fire-resistance are used for supporting the bottom or top of the vessels.

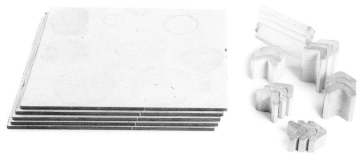

Kiln Shelves and Kiln Posts

Cone and Test-pieces

In order to measure the firing temperature and the melting temperature of ceramics, triangular cone made of a mixture of silica and alumina is used. Numbers are marked on the lower part of the side of the cone. When the tip of the cone is bent in the kiln and touches the floor, it indicates the melting temperature of the cone. In a traditional kiln, test-pieces that are made of the same clay and glaze of the vessels are used. This is a traditional means to observe the firing conditions and the melting degree of the glaze .

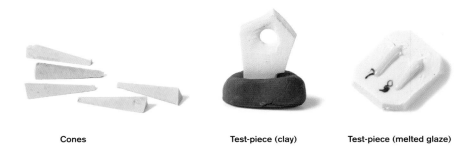

Cones   Test-piece (clay)   Test-piece (melted glaze)

Chapter 3.

Making
Celadon

Process of Making Celadon

Preparing Raw Materials

1. Collecting Raw Materials	2. Levigation	3. Kneading
Celadon clay containing 2-3% iron is collected for making celadon.	The raw material is mixed with water and strained through a sieve to sift out sand grains.	Clay is kneaded to evenly distribute the moisture and remove air bubbles.

Shaping

4-1. Shaping and Finishing (Trimming the Foot)

Shaping Various forms are shaped on the turning potter's wheel.
Finishing A thrown vessel is trimmed to make its foot.

4-2. *Sanghyeong*

Some ceramics are modeled after animals and plants.

Decoration

Bisque Firing

Glazing

5. Incising and Inlaying

Motifs are etched on the leather-hard clay body by incising technique, and the incised motifs are filled with slip by inlaying technique.

6. Bisque Firing

The dried vessels are fired at a temperature in the range of 900°C, so that impurities such as organic materials are burnt away and the glaze can be applied well.

7. Glazing

Bisque-fired vessels are dipped in the glaze to evenly cover the vessels with glaze.

Firing and Completion

8. Stacking

Glazed vessels are placed inside the saggars and stacked inside the kiln so that they can be fired evenly.

9. Second Firing

Vessels are fired at a high temperature higher than 1,200°C until the molten glaze can coat the surface evenly.

10. Cooling Down of Kiln

Using bricks and mud, stoking holes and the main hole of the fire box are sealed and allowed to cool down for more than 10 days before taking fired vessels out.

Preparing Raw Materials

The production of ceramics begins with the extraction of raw materials. And the raw material is the most basic criterion for determining the type or quality of ceramics. Celadon is made with the ingredients with a viscosity that makes it easy to form; refractoriness that maintains its shape even at high temperatures; and iron that is important in determining the color. The collected raw material is made into clay through a refining process such as levigation and kneading. Raw materials that can easily melt at a high temperature and form an even surface are prepared to make glaze. The process of collecting and preparing raw materials is an important step in determining the quality of celadon.

Collecting Raw Materials

The clay used in the celadon is highly viscous and easy to form. However, it shrinks and its color changes in a wide spectrum during firing. Celadon is

Collecting Matured Clay, Demonstrated by Bang Seung-hyeong
(Goryeo Celadon Museum)

made of clay containing 2-3% of iron and this clay is found mainly deposited in the western part of the Korean Peninsula. The deposited clay is mixed with a large amount of impurities such as organic material and iron during the formation of clay. Since the sedimentary clays are different in the viscosity of clay, iron content, distribution of sand particles and organic materials depending on the sediment layer to be collected, it is very important to manage the collection process. The earlier the clay is collected, the better the quality of the celadon is through a long period of aging. These characteristics of the sedimentary clays caused led to establish celadon production sites the near the production areas of raw materials during the Goryeo period.

Levigation

Since the collected raw materials contain various impurities such as sand grains and organic materials, the clay cannot be immediately used. The raw materials, particularly the clay, are purified through the levigation process in order to remove impurities from the raw materials.

During this process, the collected raw material is put into a levigation tank and mixed thoroughly with water. The clay slurry is delicately sieved through a fine sieve to obtain clay of fine particles. The particle size of the levigated clay varies depending on the size of the holes in the mesh of the sieve used. Since the viscosity, shrinkage, and sintering are dependent on the particle size, the mesh size of the sieve is also very important.

Sieving in the Levigation Process, Demonstrated by Bang Seung-hyeong
(Goryeo Celadon Museum)

Wedging

Small air bubbles in clay forms bubbles on the surface during firing. Refined clay through levigation process is wedged to remove the air bubbles in clay. A pug mill is generally used to wedge clay.

Pug Mill Used to Wedge Clay, Demonstrated by Jo Yu-bok (Goryeo Celadon Museum)

Shaping the Clay

For making ceramics, it is important to have clay that is excellent in plasticity for shaping and maintaining its shape. Ceramics can be shaped by various methods such as throwing on the wheel, molding, and hand building. Traditionally, the most commonly used method was wheel throwing, and most vessels such as bowl, plates, and bottles were thrown on the wheel. This method was good for making symmetrical vessels using the turning force of the wheel. However, the same shape cannot be reproduced on the wheel, so it was suitable for small quantity production. Mold casting is a method of modeling a vessel using a mold, so vessels of identical shapes can be produced in a short time using this method. Hand building is a method of modeling celadon vessels after a certain shape, particularly those that cannot be shaped on the wheel, such as water droppers and ewers, are made using this method.

Upon completing shaping ceramics by above methods, they are dried and their walls and foot are trimmed. If the ceramics have thick walls they are not only heavy for use but apt to crack when drying.

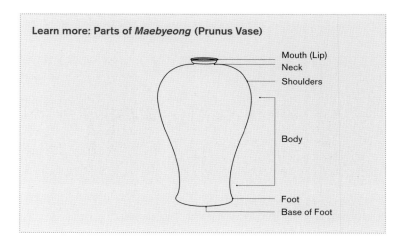

Learn more: Parts of *Maebyeong* (Prunus Vase)

Mouth (Lip)
Neck
Shoulders

Body

Foot
Base of Foot

Throwing *Maebyeong* on the Potter's Wheel

Demonstrated by Jo Ju-il (Goryeo Ceramic Museum)

Place the right amount of clay on the wheel. Wet both hands and using both center the clay on the wheel while turning the wheel.

On the turning wheel, squeeze the clay and pull it up and push it down with the palm. Repeat these two steps until and center the clay.

Center of the top of the clay is pushed with both thumbs and make a hole that is right for *maebyeong*.

Enlarge the pulled up clay by pressing the left hand on the outer surface and right hand on the interior of the hole and make a cylindrical form.

To model the clay into the shape of *maebyeong*, the cylindrical form is widened by pushing out the right hand.

When the body is completed, the mouth is formed.

Using mulgajuk, or wet leather, the mouth is smoothed.

Using a knife, the neck is formed, and its intersections with the mouth and shoulders are adjusted at the same time.

When modeling *maebyeong* is completed, a cutting wire is held and placed on the wheel.

On the slowly turning wheel, the cutting wire is pushed against the bat and run through between the bat and vessel.

Hold the lower body of the *maebyeong* with both hands and hold it up from the wheel.

Place the maebyeong on a drying board.

Finishing *Maebyeong*   Demonstrated by Jo Ju-il (Goryeo Ceramic Museum)

Place the chuck shaped to receive the *maebyeong* at the center of the wheel.

Place the half-dried *maebyeong* (about two days after shaping) on top of the chuck.

Using a trimming knife, its outer surface is smoothed, excess clay is removed, and wall thickness is evened.

The mouth is finished using a round-end knife.

The neck is delicately trimmed using a small round-end knife.

The surface is smoothed by using a sponge.

After the mouth and body are trimmed, the *maebyeong* is place upside down to trim the foot.

The lower body is smoothed and the wall thickness is evened.

The foot is trimmed using a foot knife.

The thickness of foot ring is adjusted while cutting out the foot.

The foot ring and base are smoothed using a wet sponge.

After the lower body and foot are trimmed, the *maebyeong* is moved to the drying board.

Mold Casting Bamboo Shoot-shaped Ewer

Demonstrated by Han Jin-wu (Goryeo Celadon Museum, step 1-4) and by Wi Seong-gon (Goryeo Celadon Museum, step 5-12)

Place on the table the molds for casting bamboo shoot-shaped ewer.

Assemble the molds and fill in the molds with liquefied clay or slip. (approx. 1 h. 30 min.)

Drain the excess slip from the molds and let the slip dry for 3-4 hours. When the body is modelled and separate the molds.

When the body is completed removed from the molds, it is placed on a drying board.

Place the body on the wheel and smooth the seam lines using a bamboo knife.

Remove the excess clay from the hole into which the slip was poured into and form a mouth.

Use a metal tool to mark the hole onto which a spout will be attached.

Push and turn the metal tool and make a hole for the spout.

Add slip onto the joining area of the spout using a brush.

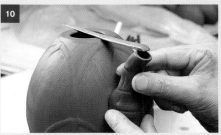

Adhere the spout to the prepared hole on the body.

Adhere the slip-cast handle onto the body using slip as a bonding agent.

Complete modeling the ewer by placing the lid on top.

Decoration

There are decoration techniques using a knife, such as incising, relief, and openwork, and techniques applied using a brush, including underglaze-iron and underglaze copper. Also, there is a technique that incorporates both incising and painting, known as underglaze iron-inlay technique. Decoration techniques using engraving knives are applied onto the surface of a vessel after it has been shaped, trimmed, and then leather-hard dried. The techniques using a brush involve painting on bisque fired vessels. Using these techniques, various patterns such as flowers, trees, birds, animals, and clouds are rendered on the surface of the celadon.

Inlay Decoration

Inlay technique is a method that involves incising motifs on the surface and filling in the cavities with slip that is different from the clay body. There is a white inlay as well as black inlay depending on the slip used.

Inlaying Decoration

Demonstrated by Ma Gwang-won (Goryeo Celadon Museum, step 1 & 5), Yun Min-hui (Goryeo Celaon Museum, step 2-4, 6-7)

White Inlaying Motifs widely used for white inlay decoration such as clouds and cranes are incised using engraving knives.

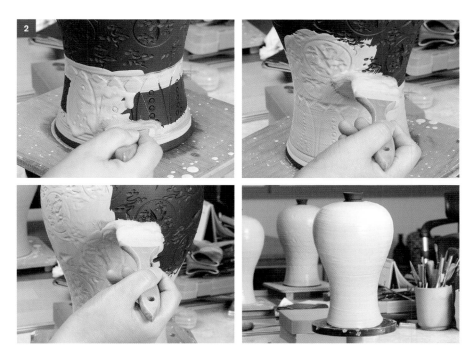

Filling in White Slip   Cavities of etched motifs are filled in with white slip using a brush from the lower to upper body. White slip is applied meticulously to avoid the forming of any air bubbles. Spraying water onto the *maebyeong* helps applying white slip evenly.

Adhere White Slip   When the white slip is half dried, it is pressed with a bamboo knife to adhere it thoroughly and also to remove any air bubbles.

Scraping White Clay   After step 4, using an incising knife, the white slip is scraped off to reveal the inlaid design.

Incising Motifs for Black Inlay   Upon completing step 5, designated parts for black inlay in incised.

Filling Red Slip   Red slip is filled in the etched cavities for black inlay using a brush.

Scraping Black Slip   When the black slip half dried, a bamboo knife is used to adhere the slip thoroughly, and an inlaying knife is used to scrape of the black slip.

Bisque Firing and Glazing

First firing of dried vessels at around 900°C is referred to as bisque firing. It is possible to manufacture clean ceramics by first firing as impurities such as organic materials contained in the dried vessels are burnt away. Also, it increases the absorbency and strength of the vessels which allows efficient application of glaze whether thick or thin.

Glazing on the bisque fired vessels not only beautifies them by the luster it creates but it also increases the strength of the wares and prevents water and chemicals from permeating. There are many ways to apply glaze, such as dipping in a glaze tank, brushing, spraying, etc., and dipping is most commonly used because it is coated most evenly.

Bisque Firing   Demonstrated by the Goryeo Celadon Museum

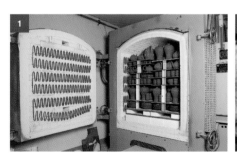

Dried vessels are bisque fired at about 900°C inside in an electric kiln before glaze is applied.

First firing burns away organic materials and other impurities contained in the unfired vessels and allows efficient application of glaze

Glazing Demonstrated by Jo Yu-bok (Goryeo Celadon Museum)

Bisque fired *maebyeong* are brought near the glaze tank. Holding the mouth and base, the vase is dipped into the tank.

The *maebyeong* is thoroughly applied by turning it inside the tank.

Glaze is allowed inside the *maebyeong* in order to glaze the interior.

When glazing is finished, the *maebyeong* is taken out from the mouth.

The *maebyeong* stands upright when removed from the tank.

Excess glaze is drained back into the tank by turning *maebyeong* upside down.

Unglazed parts that were held by fingers while dipping are glazed using a brush, and the glazed surface is evened using a knife.

lazed vessels of different types are grouped respectively on plank boards

Firing and Completion

Glazed vessels are placed inside saggars and stacked in a kiln so that they can be fired evenly at a constant temperature.

In the case of celadon, bisque fired and glazed wares are stacked in a kiln and fired for the second time at a high temperature of about 1,200°C. There are reduction firing and oxidation firing in the second firing. In reduction firing, oxygen is eliminated or restricted inside the kiln so that the oxygen of iron oxide in clay and glaze is removed, which creates a reduction atmosphere inside the kiln. The green color of celadon glaze is made possible in this atmosphere. In order to develop a reduction atmosphere, oxygen inside the kiln is eliminated slowly to the minimum by controlling the kiln chimney starting from a temperature of about 900°C and to 1260°C. On the other hand, in oxidation firing, which is when enough oxygen is supplied inside the kiln, celadon displays a brown hue.

....

Stacking   Demonstrated by the Goryeo Celadon Museum

Before stacking, test-pieces are placed in the spy-holes so that they can be checked during firing.

Alumina powder is coated on the interior wall of the saggar and then glazed vessels are placed inside.

Inside the kiln, refractory bricks are arranged at regular intervals on the floor of firing chambers. Outside the kiln, saggars are moved to near the doorway of each chamber and they are passed to a person inside for stacking.

Saggared ceramics are stacked from the back of the kiln considering the flow of flame, the type of vessel and size

After stacking saggars from the end of the kiln, refractory bricks are arranged on the floor at regular intervals in front and saggars are stacked on top.

Second Firing   Demonstrated by the Goryeo Celadon Museum

After stacking is completed three side doorways are closed first with refractory bricks and then completely sealed with clay.

When closing the doorways, a stoking hole is made by leaving one brick unsealed with clay so that it could be removed whenever stoking is needed.

Firewood is put into the stoking hole and temperature is raised slowly inside the kiln. When the temperature of the furnace reaches about 1,000°C, potters stop feeding firewood and move to the side doorways.

More firewood is put into the kiln through the side stoking holes to raise the temperature inside. When each firing chamber reaches 1260°C, potters take out the test-pieces from the spy-holes and check the colors and conditions of the glaze.

Fire the kiln is fueled, spy-holes and the main stoking hole in front are completely sealed with bricks and clay to black the air from permeating.

After the second firing is finished, the kiln is left to cool down for about 10 days. When the kiln has cooled down, main stoking hole and side doorways are opened and celadon wares are take out from the saggars.

Chapter 4

Enjoying
Korean
Celadon

Goryeo's Noble Taste and Elegance

For about a century during the reigns of King Munjong (1046-1082) to King Injong (1122-1146) in the Goryeo Dynasty, the art culture of Goryeo has thrived. This culture, which is clearly distinguished from the Unified Silla and the Joseon Dynasty, is a colorful and original culture of aristocratic society. Among them, crafts used almost perfect technology, showing full practicality and excellent formability, and bringing up the stage to be considered a country of crafts.

In the literature, there are records of leisure activities that were mainly enjoyed by the bureaucrats and literary classes. In the *Saryunjeonggi* (四輪亭記) written by Yi Gyu-bo (1168-1241), known as the representative literary man of the Goryeo Dynasty, there is a phrase that reads "In the summer, we sit down in the garden with our guests, lie down and sit down and drink. We play *go* and play the *geomungo*. It ends as we please when the day falls. This is the pleasure of the man of leisure." As in this text, literary writers in the Goryeo Dynasty invited a couple of close writers to a secluded pavilion, and enjoyed their leisure time by drinking tea and wine, playing the *geomungo*, playing *go* and composing poems together. In particular, the brush stand, pencil, and other stationery needed for composing poetry and sentence construction were made into celadon. Thus, it can be seen that celadon stationery was cherished by the literati.

In addition to the stationery, pillows, incense burners, a celadon chair, and many other items were made of Goryeo celadon so as to enrich people's leisure time. Even the roof tiles were made in celadon, which suggests how high-class life was pursued at that time. These celadon artifacts reflect the noble taste of the Goryeo people who appreciated poetry and painting.

Celadon Incense Burner with Openwork Design,
National Treasure No. 95, Goryeo, 12th century, H. 15.3cm,
National Museum of Korea
This incense burner is comprised of a globular cover through which
smoke can escape; a lotus-like body, and a base supported by three
rabbit-shaped legs. This is a functional object made up of three
parts of different shapes, and diverse decorating techniques were
employed, including incising, relief, openwork, inlaying, and paste-
on-paste.

Celadon Water Dropper in the Shape of Mother and Baby Monkeys, National Treasure No. 270, Goryeo, 12th century, H. 9.8cm, Kansong Museum
Only a few extant celadon water droppers are modelled like monkeys, and this is the only piece made in the shape of a mother and a baby monkey. There is a one-diameter wide opening for adding water, and a spout with 0.3 wide in diameter is made on the baby monkey's head. Even the fingers of both monkeys are made naturally by carving between the fingers, and their eyes and noses have been marked with black dots. A mother monkey is hugging a wining baby expressing the love between mother and baby. Jade-colored glaze has well fused with the body, and air bubbles make the glaze appear soft.

Celadon Brush Stand with Openwork Lotus Scroll Design and Dragon Head-shaped Ornament,
Treasure No. 1932, Goryeo, 12th century, H. 8.8cm, National Museum of Korea
There are only a few extant celadon brush stands unlike the other writing accoutrements such as ink pot and water droppers, many of which are high quality. This ornate celadon brush holder demonstrates exceptional sculptural expertise employing different methods of decoration. Each of the dragon heads is carved in meticulous detail with a distinctive mane, frills, fangs, and scales. The mythical dragons were a symbol of royal authority, and lotus flowers were also an icon of Buddhism. This elaborately decorated piece was made for the royal court or aristocrats. This is not only a rare item but exceptional for the aesthetic form and glaze color that make it a true masterpiece of Goryeo celadon.

Celadon Spittoon with Peony Scroll Design in Relief, Goryeo, 12th century, H. 9.5cm,
National Museum of Korea
This spittoon features peony scrolls in relief on the dish-like upper body and on the exterior wall of its pot-shaped lower body. The design stands out as its contours are broadly carved out. Translucent grayish-blue glaze containing minor bubbles covers it entirely, and there are thick fine cracks dispersed on the surface. There are spur marks on the outer bottom.

Celadon Pillow with Inlaid Peony, Crane, and Cloud Design, Goryeo, 12th century, H. 12.7cm,
National Museum of Korea
This is the most sophisticated surviving celadon pillow. It was built with six slabs. The pillow is tapered in the middle which resulted in the visual effect and function of the pillow. Its both ends are bordered with lotus leaves. Each side is reverse inlaid with scrolls on the background. In the middle of the up and bottom sides are black inlaid with a circle and cranes and clouds are inlaid inside.

Goryeo Celadon for Tea Drinking

Since the early Goryeo Dynasty, tea which was introduced at the end of the Silla Kingdom had been widely consumed in the king's bounty, offering diplomatic contributions to temples as well as the national rituals. Tea culture was one of the high-class cultures enjoyed by upper class people such as aristocrats and monks. As time went by, it became generalized and became a daily life beverage and tea drinking came to be enjoyed by the general people. The taste of tea and the effect of drinking tea are the reasons why it became widely popular, but the act of brewing tea is also one of the great pleasures. Drinking tea and having a decent conversation was a common custom of the upper reaches of the Gaegyeong city.

In Goryeo royal family, there is a ceremonial ritual called the *jinda* ceremony for offering a king a tea for various events including lotus lantern event, offering rituals to local deities, and receiving foreign envoys. In order to take charge of this, they even set up a government office called a *dabang*. The general people enjoyed tea in a tea house called a *dajeom*. With the proliferation of tea culture, tea utensils were developed naturally. The general people enjoyed tea in a tea house called multipurpose teahouse. With the proliferation of tea culture, tea utensils were developed naturally. It was also good for celadon to drink tea and drink well.

Celadon Cup with Inlaid Chrysanthemum Design,
Goryeo, H. 7.9cm, National Museum of Korea
This cylindrical cup narrows toward the mouth and has a foot attached. A band of fretwork is white inlaid on the upper end, and on the lower end are black and white inlaid with lotus leaves against a band of white inlay. Four four-petal flowers with black and white inlay outlines and a chrysanthemum inside adorn the four sides of the cup. Between the flowers are inlaid two chrysanthemum sprays. It is applied with greenish light jade-color glaze.

Celadon Lobed Bowl with Peony Design in Relief,
Goryeo, 12th century, H. 6.1cm,
National Museum of Korea
This bowl is mold-impressed with peonies and their
contours are carved to make them stand out. Mold-
impressing technique has a limitation in expressing fine
detailed lines, so mold-impressing is usually employed
together with incising technique.

**Celadon Cup and Stand with Inlaid Chrysanthemum
Design,** Goryeo, 13th century, H. 12.6cm,
National Museum of Korea

During the Goryeo period, metal cups and stands of this
shape and design were popular. In particular, this set of
cup and stand is foliated because they were modelled
after metal counterparts. The cup is flower-shaped, and
below the mouth are incised scrolls. Each rim is inlaid with
chrysanthemum. The stand is incised with a chrysanthemum
at its upper center and on the rim are also chrysanthemums
in relief.

Celadon Ewer with Incised Cucumber and Vine Design, Goryeo, 12th century, H. 19cm,
National Museum of Korea
This ewer has a spherical body with a spout and handle attached. The handle has been repaired. The front and back of the body are loosely incised with a plant of the gourd family. Leaves and fruits are done in demi-relief and veins are rendered in fine incised lines. The foot is low and glaze has been wiped off the foot. There are spur marks of refractory clay and sand in seven places.

Jade-colored Celadon, The Best under Heaven

The emergence of Goryeo celadon was definitely through importing the techniques from Yue kilns of the Five Dynasties. However, at some point the quality of Goryeo celadon began to surpass that of Chinese celadon. In a travelog of the Song China envoy, *Xuanhe fengshi Gaoli tujing* (宣和奉使高麗圖經), Xu Jing (徐兢, 1091-1153) stated that "the Goryeo people refer to the blue or green of their ceramics as '*bisaek*.' In recent years, these pieces have recently been made with great skill, and the luster has become especially fine." Also, in *Brocade on the Sleeve*, a book written about ten masterpieces by a Chinese connoisseur whose sobriquet is Taiping Laoren, there is a phrase that reads "Goryeo jade-color is the first under heaven." Here, the jade-color, or *bisaek*, is another designation of Chinese celadon. China was the first to produce celadon, but they regarded Goryeo celadon as the best of its kind. Such contemporary references bear witness to how impressed the Chinese were by the jade-color of Goryeo celadon.

Through achieving the jade color and developing sophisticated, elegant form, the people of Goryeo had elevated the value of their celadon to the highest level. *Celadon Melon-shaped Bottle*, discovered in the tomb of King Injong (r. 1122-1146), is an example showing the excellence of Goryeo celadon in its jade-colored glaze, balanced proportion, and skillful transformation of metal ware into celadon. This melon-shaped bottle is built thin with perfection proportions, and in particular it represents the jade-color glaze of the mid-Goryeo period.

Celadon Melon-shaped Bottle, National Treasure No. 94, Goryeo, 12th century, H. 22.6cm,
National Museum of Korea

This bottle is a representative piece of the 12th century Goryeo celadon during its golden age. This was unearthed from the tomb of King Injong at Jangdan-gun in Gyeonggi-do Province along with a book of posthumous name that bears the inscription of "6th year Hwangtong (1146)". The bottle has a melon-shaped body, a flaring, pleated foot, and a mouth with eight lobes. There are three lines on the neck and no further decoration has been applied. This type of bottle was imported from Song China, but it appears more elegant and refined in proportion. Translucent grayish blue celadon glaze is evenly coated. Its form, glaze, and clay body demonstrates that it is a work of the golden age of Goryeo celadon.

Celadon *Maebyeong* with Incised Lotus Scroll Design, National Treasure No. 97, Goryeo, 12th century, H. 43.9cm, National Museum of Korea

This is a classic example of Goryeo celadon *maebyeong*, or prunus vase, with a small yet sturdy mouth, swollen shoulders, a slim waist, and a flaring bottom. The entire body is incised with large lotus and scrolls, and the scrolls were rendered in demi-relief to make them more visible. In the earlier stage, the incised lines were sharp and fine, but during the golden age of Goryeo celadon (the mid-12th century) they became rather thick and done in demi-relief. Clear and light-green glaze with a grayish blue tint is applied evenly on the entire vase.

Celadon Bamboo Shoot-shaped Ewer, Treasure No. 1931, Goryeo, 12th century, H. 23.5cm, National Museum of Korea
This ewer is in the shape of a bamboo shoot, a popular subject for *sanghyeong* celadon, which is modelled after certain physical shapes. Its body, spout, handle, and other parts are all incorporated naturally in a perfectly balanced form. Jade-colored glaze is evenly applied and with almost no crackles. The glazed surface is impeccable and lustrous. This is a fine example of plain celadon.

Inlaid Celadon, Quintessence of Goryeo Celadon

Goryeo celadon can be characterized by the jade-colored glaze, the formative beauty of *sanghyeong* celadon modelled after certain physical shapes, and inlaid designs incorporating different materials yielding an ornate yet lyrical atmosphere. In particular, Goryeo inlaid celadon is a remarkable achievement that is unprecedented in the history of ceramics.

Inlaying requires carving designs on the clay body and filling cavities with different types of clay. This technique was also employed in decorating lacquer ware with mother-of-pearl or in metalwork. Adopting such method onto ceramics was from the creative idea of Goryeo potters. Arduous efforts were made required for achieving this inlaying technique. It has been widely believed that inlaying technique was applied soon after the production of celadon began. However it was employed only partially and was in full swing from the twelfth century.

Many different patterns were created by this method. There were examples with picturesque designs like a piece of painting or with very ornate designs repeatedly using a particular pattern. The inlaid celadon is a phenomenal invention in the history of ceramics even by the technique itself, but it is of great significance in that the patterns rendered by this technique carried the heart of Goryeo people of that time. The crane and cloud design in a spacious space of the jade-color glaze, which seem to represent the skies, was the most popular motif of the Goryeo celadon. The pattern was a symbol of auspiciousness and the dignity and long history of a thousand years.

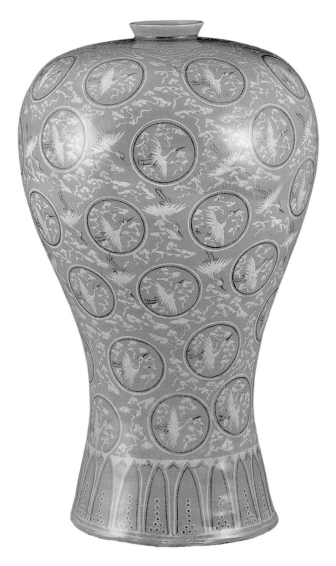

Celadon *Maebyeong* with Inlaid Cloud and Crane Design, National Treasure No. 68, Goryeo, 13th century, H. 42.1cm, Kansong Museum

This *maenyeong*, or prunus vase, is inlaid with clouds and cranes on the body. Inside the black and white inlaid circles are inlaid cranes soaring up while outside the circles are cranes landing. Cranes are flying in different directions seemingly pursuing the freedom from the structured composition by extending the space in all directions overcoming the restrictions of the closed space of ceramic ware. This is a creative and skillful work of art in expanding and challenging the means of expression.

Celadon Jar with Inlaid Peony Design, National Treasure No. 98, Goryeo, 12th century, H. 19.8cm,
National Museum of Korea
During the Goryeo period bronze wares were also used widely used, along with celadon ware. Some celadon wares
were modelled after bronze wares. This is one such example. The two handles in the shape of an animal were
inspired by the bronze counterparts. This is a rare piece in that is large in size and decoration. Peony is white inlaid
and outlined with black inlaid lines. Fine incised lines were used to express veins on flower petals. Clear greenish
gray-blue celadon is applied thin overall. The glaze is transparent and lustrous.

Celadon Bowl with Silver Lip, Lotus Scroll Design in relief and Inlaid Peony Design,
National Treasure No. 253, Goryeo, 12th century, H. 7.9cm, National Museum of Korea
This is a unique piece in that its mouth rim is cover with silver lining. On the inner bottom circle is carved a
flower, and the inner wall is mold-impressed with lotus scrolls. The outer surface is inlaid with peony.
This is a transitional ware between plain and inlaid celadon as the inlaid design is rendered rather modestly.

Celadon Gourd-shaped Ewer with Inlaid Peony Scroll Design, National Treasure No. 116,
Goryeo, 12th century, H. 34.3cm, National Museum of Korea
The lower body is decorated in reverse inlay with schematized peony design. Fine incised lines are used to express
the veins in flower petals and leaves. The upper body is inlaid with clouds and cranes. The spout is decorated with
white paste on paste. The glaze is jade-colored with a gray-blue tint and is lustrous yet soft.

Celadon Lobed Bowl with Inlaid *Bonghwang* and Cloud Design, Goryeo, H 8.6cm, National Museum of Korea

This is a flower-shaped bowl richly decorated with a mythical bird known as *bonghwang* and clouds. *Bonghwang* and dragons were symbols of high class, so such designs were used in high-quality wares. This bowl is mainly decorated by white inlay except for the heads of *bonghwang* and crane and cranes' legs, which were done in black inlay.

Celadon Melon-shaped Bottle with Inlaid Peony and Chrysanthemum Design, National Treasure No. 114, Goryeo, late 12th-13th century, H. 25.6cm, National Museum of Korea
This bottle has a melon-shaped body with eight ribbed vertical sides. Black and white inlaid chrysanthemum and peony sprays alternate in the ribbed sides. On the lower end of the body are reverse inlaid lotus leaves, and a band of *ruyi* heads encircle the shoulders.

Celadon with Poetry

During the Goryeo period, the nobles enjoyed a free and leisurely life, and they enjoyed the taste of drinking wine in a celadon. During the Goryeo Dynasty, there was a government office called Yangonseo, which managed the liquor and sweet rice drink required for royal and national ceremonies. In the second year of the reign of King Seongjong (983), six taverns including Seongye, Akbin, Yeollyeong, Aek, and Huibin were constructed and operated.

In the latter half of the eleventh century, during the reign of King Injong, when Goryeo reinstated the trade with the Song Dynasty, the Goryeo made golden wine vessels (金酒器) to offer as a gift. In addition, according to the record, King Injong gave Kim Bu-Sik a golden wine vessel to celebrate completion of *Samguksagi* (History of the Three Kingdoms) compilation. Thus, the alcoholic beverage was recognized as an important food along with tea, because it was used for ritual ceremonies or royal family service. In this way, the taste of naturalness is well presented in sophisticated celadon culture, and the poems carved on the surfaces of celadon bottles and kettles convey the romance and lyricism related to alcohol.

Celadon Bowl with Inscription of "三盃詩" and Inlaid Scroll Design, Goryeo, 12th-13th century, H. 8.1cm, National Museum of Korea
A band of white inlaid scrolls circles around the outer rim of the mouth, and a quatrain with five characters is black inlaid vertically below it.

三盃詩	A poem for drinking three cups of wine
天許方四盃	If the sky permits, I could drink the fourth cup
三盃皆已得	I drank all three cups
何逢方二杯	How did I drink the second one
亦足含笑盃	Of course, leisurely, smiling
方四笑盃	The fourth cup is also with a smile.

Celadon Bottle with Inscription of Poem,
Goryeo, 13th century, H. 34.9cm,
National Museum of Korea

何處難忘酒　It's hard not to drink wherever it is
靑門送別多　People separate at the gate of capital
斂襟收涕淚　Adjusting their clothes they wipe
　　　　　　their tears
促馬聽笙歌　Urging the horse, I listen to the flute
煙樹灞陵岸　Trees with clouds in Pareung Hill
風塵長樂坡　That is endless happiness of life
此時無逸盞　If there is not a drink then
爭奈去留何　What would appease the separation

Celadon Ewer with Inscription of Poem and Inlaid Scroll Design, Goryeo, 12th century, H. 24.1cm,
National Museum of Korea
暫入新豊市　Briefly stopped by in Xinfeng county (famous for wine)
猶聞舊酒香　Smelled the old, stale wine
把琴沽一醉　Playing the zither I buy drinks and get drunk
盡日臥垂楊　I lay down under the willow tree until the sun goes down

Celadon Bottle with Inscription of Poem and Incised Lotus Scroll Design, Goryeo, 12th century, H. 38.8cm, National Museum of Korea

This gourd-shaped bottle is densely decorated with lotus scroll in demi-relief to make the design stand out but the veins in petals and leaves are incised with fine lines. An ogival-shaped window is made on either side of the lower body and the following poem of a quatrain with seven characters is black inlaid inside.

細鏤金花碧玉壺　The beautiful blue wine bottle is decorated with golden flowers
豪家應是喜提壺　The bottle was likely cherished by an affluent family
須知賀老乘清興　When He Zhi Zhang was feeling good
抱向春深醉鏡湖　He was probably drunk holding this bottle at a retreat in the late spring

Lifelike *Sanghyeong* Celadon

Many extant *sanghyeong* celadon wares reflect the aesthetics and taste of the upper classes of the Goryeo Dynasty. *Sanghyeong* celadons, modeled after certain physical shapes, were also produced in China; however, they differed from their Goryeo counterparts in terms of function, model subjects, consumers, and transparency of the glaze. Goryeo produced celadon with unique features. While adopting the styles of Chinese *sanghyeong* celadon, those of Goryeo developed independently by choosing the material and types suitable for consumers of that era. Goryeo wanted to develop their unique features of celadon while accepting the advanced Chinese objects and techniques, and they had finally achieved establishing their distinct formative characters as seen in the following examples; *Celadon Water Dropper in the Shape of Mother and Baby Monkeys* (see p.108), *Celadon Pomegranate-shaped Ewer* (see p.132), *Celadon Water Dropper in the Shape of a Young Girl*, and *Celadon Boy-shaped Water Dropper*. *Sanghyeong* celadon have been made in the shapes of animals such as ducks, mandarin ducks, lions, mythical animals such as *girin*, *bonghwang*, dragon, and sea dragon, and monkeys. Also, they were made in the shape of plants including pomegranate, peaches, and lotus; and human figures including boys, the Buddha, bodhitsattvas, and Daoist figures. Lifelike *sanghyeong* celadon wares were made in the above-mentioned forms, and surviving examples show that this is another remarkable achievement of Goryeo celadon.

(left) Celadon Water Dropper in the Shape of a Young Girl, Goryeo, 12th century, H. 11.1cm, Oriental Ceramics Museum, Osaka
(right) Celadon Water Dropper in the Shape of a Boy, Goryeo, 12th century, H. 11cm, Oriental Ceramics Museum, Osaka

Celadon Incense Burner with Lion-shaped Lid, National Treasure No. 60, Goryeo, early 12th century, H. 21.2cm, National Museum of Korea
This incense burner has a lion-shaped lid through which smoke can escape. In the case of the lid, another tier was formed on the upper side, and a lion is placed on it. The lion decorated on the lid is slightly shifted to the right from the center, which seems to have slipped while glazing after the lion was carved and put on the lid. The crouching back legs, big round eyes highlighted with underglaze iron black, lowered ears, and the tail extending to the back all look familiar. The beautiful and unique jade-colored glaze and sophisticated form of this piece reflect the high-quality craftsmanship of Goryeo craftwork.

Celadon Ewer in the Shape of a Fish-dragon, National Treasure No. 61, Goryeo, 12th century, H. 24.3cm, National Museum of Korea

This ewer is in the shape of an imaginary animal, a fish-dragon, which is leaping up. The fish –dragon has the head of dragon and the body of a fish. The spout follows the shape of a dragon's head, and teeth, fins and tail ends are added with white paste on paste. The hair and fins on the face are very elaborately rendered. Scales on the body stand out. Two large rake-like fins are expressed on the front and back. The handle is shaped like a lotus stem, naturally hanging over the body, and the lid is made to mimic the tail of the fish. The faint incised lines on the fins and floral patterns show skilled workmanship.

Celadon Pomegranate-shaped Water Dropper,
Goryeo, 12th century, H. 8cm,
National Museum of Korea
This water dropper is in the shape of a
pomegranate with a monkey sitting on it. Such
types of vessels were both decorative and
practical at the same time. The calyx on the top
has an opening to pour in the water and the
monkey's mouth is the spout. The foot is in the
form of a stem. On the back of the pomegranate
are densely inlaid bit white dots, expressing the
ripe fruit. The monkey's eyes are marked with
red clay. It is covered rather thickly with greenish
jade-colored glaze.

Celadon Duck-shaped Water Dropper, National Treasure No. 74, Goryeo, 12th century, H. 8cm,
Kansong Museum
A duck floating on the water is holding a lotus stem in its mouth. A lotus leaf and bud are on the back of its body,
and an opening is made among them. The opening is capped with the bud-shaped knob. The spout is made on the
right side of the duck's mouth and is believed to be connected to the bud at the tip of the lotus stem. But this part
is damaged now, so it is difficult to know the original form. Even the feathers are incised realistically and naturally.
The appropriate size of the water dropper and skillful techniques for carving, and the subtle color of the glaze all
show aspects of the aristocratic society of Goryeo.

Celadon Pomegranate-shape Ewer, Goryeo, 12th century, H. 18.3cm, National Museum of Korea
While most ewers were shaped on the potter's wheel and applied patterns on its surface, this example is made by joining four pomegranates. The ewer is shaped in a stable triangular form by placing one pomegranate on top of three.

Celadon Taoist Figure-shaped Ewer, National Treasure No. 167, Goryeo, 12th-13th century, H. 28cm, National Museum of Korea
This is a celadon pitcher shaped like a Taoist figure upholding a fairyland pear. An opening is made on top of the figure's head for pouring the water into, but its cap is missing. The pitcher has a handle attached to its back. It is not known whether this was actually used.

Reproduction and Reinterpretation of Goryeo Celadon

The beautiful jade-color of Goryeo celadon is the color of serenity. In the calm and clear tons of grayish blue, the emotions of serenity are felt. It is probably because of the emotions stemming from the color of Goryeo celadon that quietness is mentioned when discussing the characteristics of Korean beauty.

Goryeo celadon was recreated through the efforts of some potters who dreamed of recreating Goryeo celadon in the 1950s, though the Goryeo celadon turned naturally into the *buncheong* celadon during the Joseon Dynasty. The representative figure is Hae Gang Yoo Kun-hyong, who led the succession of the Goryeo celadon tradition in Icheon, Gyeonggi-do. Since then, several potters have participated in the celadon work, and in the 1980s dozens of kilns came to produce celadon.

Celadon, which was produced only by Korea and China in world pottery history, is a unique tradition of Korea and it is a genre that can best showcase the Korean ceramics tradition. Therefore, the modernization of the celadon is a very important task. After the revival of the celadon, celadon work was actively performed, but the modern celadon work is relatively weak.

Traditional celadon has mainly originated from the work of replicating the Goryeo celadon masterpieces designated as national treasures or treasures. In the meantime, progress has been made in various aspects such as sculpture technique, molding and glaze. Gradually, they tried to make their own new celadon from cloning and developed into various facets. Currently, the traditional celadon has been succeeded by the master craftsmen.

Celadon porcelains with contemporary formality are also being produced by budding potters. They use a modern design while utilizing the unique feel of the celadon, and utilize the deep and mysterious feeling of celadon in a formative way.

Celadon *Maebyeong* with Openwork Dragon and Cloud Design, Kim Bok-han (Master of Korea),
2013, H. 45cm
Kim Bok-han from Masan, Gyeongsangnam-do began making ceramics with the idea of realizing the color
of jade-color. Decorated with openwork design of dragons and clouds, this was made with celadon clay and
celadon glaze and fired in oxidation atmosphere at 1245°C.

Celadon *Maebyeong* with Inlaid and Sgraffito Dragon Design, Jo Se-yeon (Master of Icheon City), 2013, H. 45cm

Celadon *Girin*-shaped Incense Burner, Kwon Tae-hyun (Master of Korea), 2014, H. 17cm

Celadon Long-necked Bottle with Openwork Design, Yang Myung-hwan, 2009, H. 32cm
Yang Myung-hwan works in Gwangju, Gyeonggi-do Province, and has a great skill of making celadon with a brilliant color of glaze and openwork. His celadon displays a deep and mysterious color.

Celadon Flattened Bottle with Incised and Raised Linear Design, Choi In-kyu (Master of Icheon City), 2011, H. 30cm

Choi has worked at Haegang Goryeo Celadon Research Institute and made celadon for more than 45 years. He has created his unique technique of making incised and raised designs at the same time. This bottle is a good example of such technique. This is a modern interpretation of flattened bottle. It is simple and elegant.

Celadon *Maebyeong* Revers Inlaid with Grape Vines and Boys, Kim Jong-ho (Master of Icheon City), 2013, H. 45cm

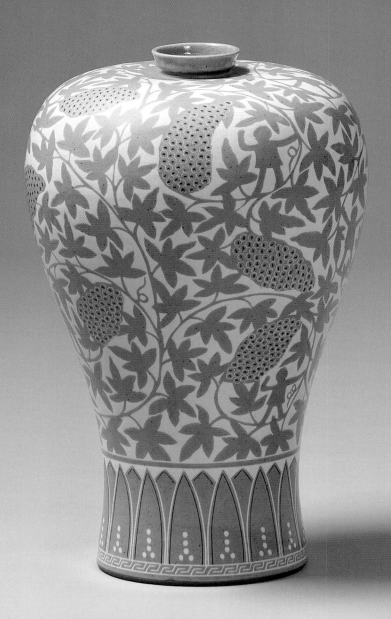

Celadon Jar with Rainbow Peony Deisgn, Kim Sung-tae, 2017, H. 50cm

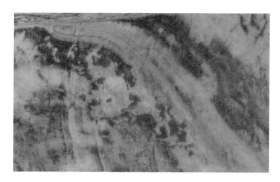

Celadon Square Bottle with Marble Design, Yoo Kwang-yul (Master of Korea), 2011, H. 12cm
While Yoo Kun-hyong (sobriquet Haegang) created the golden age of traditional celadon that interpreted the Goryeo celadon, his son Yoo Kwang-yul challenged in creating modernized pieces. This is a horizontal bottle made with the unique traditional marbling design incorporated with contemporary sense of design.

Celadon Jar with Double Layer of Openwork Design, Kim Se-yong (Master of Korea), 2011, H. 22cm
Kim played a crucial role in creating traditional celadon wares. His works are excellent in carving, shaping and in the color of glaze but mostly in openwork. His celadon wares with openwork are based on traditional wares but in contemporary sense of design. This jar is double-walled and decorated with openwork chrysanthemum design.

Celadon Three-legged Incense Burner, Lee Dong-ha, 2010, H. 13cm
Lee Dong-ha is a contemporary ceramic artist who concentrates on creating celadon wares reinterpreting and adding traditional celadon elements. Lee's celadon color is clear, soft, and warm.

Celadon Basin with Fruit Design, Kim Pan-ki, 2013, H. 11cm
Kim Pan-ki started with traditional celadon work and developed into a modern celadon. Kim trained celadon making by creating and understanding traditional works that differ from those who received formative lessons. This work is a large work with a diameter of 30cm or more. It is simple and bold, but it contains a very sophisticated sense of detail.

Celadon Cylindrical Bottle with Marbling *Bosanghwa* Scroll Design
Kim Yu-sung, 2016, H. 57.5cm
This bottle is mainly decorated with traditional designs including *bosanghwa* (medallion flower) and scrolls. Its background is black and white inlaid in many layers and carved to create the marbling effect. The incorporation of *bosanghwa* scrolls and marbling design in the background create an all the more ornate and colorful vessel.

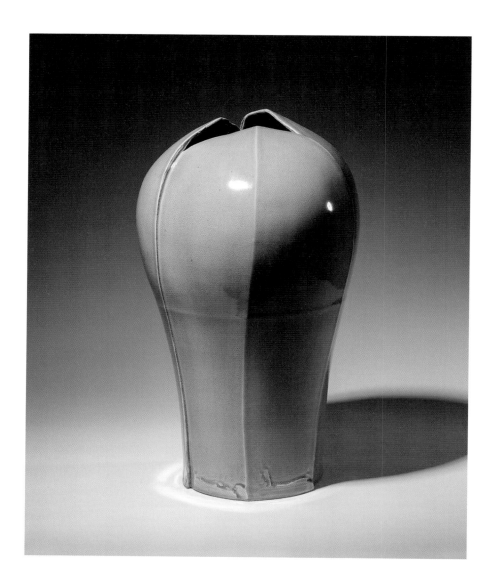

Flower Petal Jar, Lee Eun-bum, 2012, H. 54cm, courtesy of the Korea Ceramic Foundation
Lee Eun-bum is one of the ceramic artists who is pioneering contemporary celadon. He was trained in making traditional works, so his works display Korean aesthetics found in traditional wares. At the same time, his work is highly modern in shape, showing the direction of modern celadon. This work was transformed after thrown on the wheel. The clay on the bottom has been treated artistically, and the shoulders and above display the tension like the flowering petals.

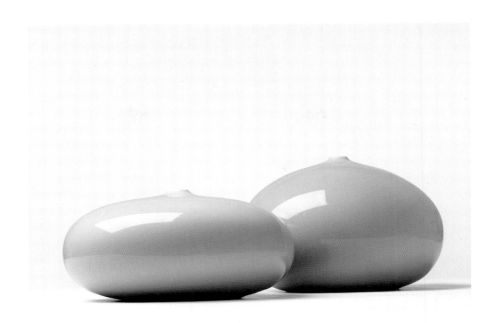

Waterdrop, Lee Ka-jin, 2013, H. 25cm (left), 33cm (right), courtesy of the Korea Ceramic Foundation
Lee Ka-jin is a ceramic artist who works with celadon glaze and reinterprets the deep and mysterious colors of the celadon. For her, the most important formative element of Goryeo celadon is the color, and her works maximize the artistic aura of the celadon color. The incorporation of minimal form, such as water droplets, and celadon glaze color reveals a very beautiful aesthetic world.

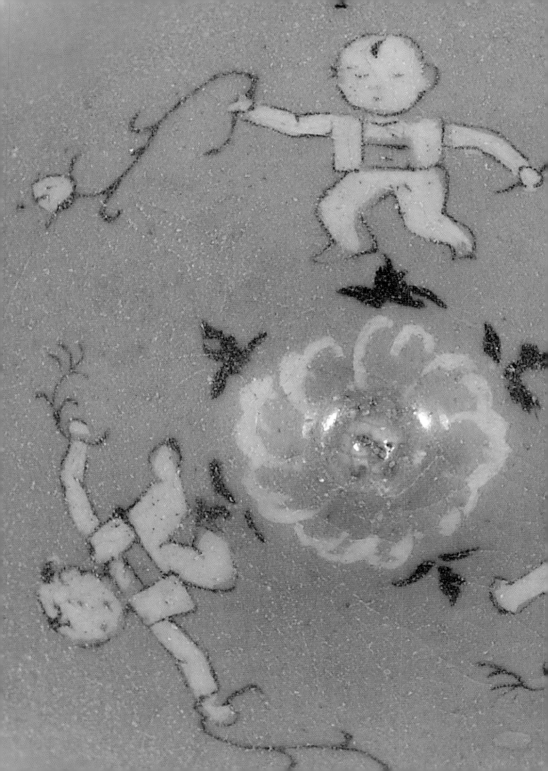

Appendix

Master Craftsmen

National Intangible Cultural Heritage (as of December 2017)

Designation No	Title	Title Holder	Designation Date
No. 105	*Sagijang* (Ceramic Making)	Kim Jeong-ok (Mungyeong, Gyeongsangbuk-do Province)	Jul. 01, 1996

Regional Intangible Cultural Heritage (as of December 2017)

Region	Designation No.	Title	Title Holder	Designation Date
Jeollanam-do Province (Gangjin-gun)	No. 36	*Cheongjajang* (Celadon Making)	Yi Yong-hee	Feb. 13, 2004
Jeollabuk-do Province (Buan-gun)	No. 29	*Sagijang* (Ceramic Making, Celadon)	Yi Eun-gyu	Sep. 10, 2004
Jeollabuk-do Province (Gimje)	No. 29	*Sagijang* (Ceramic Making, Buncheong ware)	Jang Dong-guk	Dec. 28, 2015
Chungcheongbuk-do (Danyang-gun)	No. 10	*Sagijang*	Seo Dong-gyu	Oct. 25, 2002
Gyeongsangbuk-do (Sangju)	No. 32	*Sagijang* (Ceramic Making, *Buncheong* Ware, White Porcelain)	Yi Hak-cheon	Jul. 10, 2006
Gyeongsangbuk-do (Mungyeong)	No. 32-2	*Sagijang* (Ceramic Making, Black-glazed Ware)	Cheon Han-bong	Oct. 26, 2006
Gyeongsangbuk-do (Mungyeong)	No. 32-4	*Sagijang* (Ceramic Making, White Porcelain)	Kim Yeong-sik	Aug. 14, 2017
Gyeonggi-do Province (Icheon)	No. 41	*Sagijang* (Ceramic Making, White Porcelain)	Seo Gwang-su	Feb. 07, 2005
Gyeonggi-do Province (Yeoju)	No. 41-1	*Sagijang* (Ceramic Making, Blue-and-White Ware)	Han Sang-gu	Feb. 07, 2005
Gyeonggi-do Province (Gwangju)	No. 41-2	*Sagijang* (Ceramic Making, *Buncheong* Ware)	Bak Sang-jin	Jun. 17, 2011

Craft & Design Map

Gyeonggi-do

Gangwon-do

Paju Brass Master / Bow and Arrow Master

Goyang Paper Restoration Master
Buddhistic Drawing Master / Musical Instrument Master

Bucheon
Bow and Arrow Master

Gapyeong
Hanji Paper Master

Guri Stone Cutting Master
Seongnam
Decorative Knot Master

Hoengseong Gangwon
Hoengseong Traditional
Porcelain Training Center

Seoul
Decorative Knot Master
Needle Work Master
House-building Master
Ox Horn Inlay Master
Metal Thread Inlay Master
Gilt Master / Dancheong Master
Gat Master
Calligraphic Engraving Master
Engraving Master / Brass Master
Roof Tiling Master
Joinery Master
Musical Instrument Master
Lacquer Master
Leather Shoe Master
Embroidery Master
Seoul Learning Center for National
Intangible Cultural Heritage

Incheon
Incheon Learning Center
for National Intangible
Cultural Heritage Bow
and Arrow Master
Ox Horn Inlay Master
Sedge Weaving Master

Gwangju Ceramic Ware Master / Dancheong Master

Gunpo Brassware Master

Wonju Najeon Master

Icheon Ceramic Ware Master

Yeoju Ceramic Ware Master / Earthenware Master / Ceramic Ware Master / Woodcarving Master

Suwon Stone Cutting Master
Suwon Learning Center for National Intangible Cultural Heritage

Anseong Brassware Master

Chungcheongbuk-do

Danyang Ceramic Ware Master /
Learning Center for Porcelain

Jincheon Cast Iron Master
Jincheon Learning Center for Cast Iron

Goesan Metal Type Master

Yecheon Bow and Arrow Master

Chungcheongnam-do

Cheongju Cheongju Ancient
Printing Culture Learning Center
of Frame, Scroll and Screen
Learning Center of Earthenware

Mungyeong Ceramic Ware Master /
Ceramic Ware Master / Brassware Master

Sangju Ceramic Ware Master

Yeongdeok
Learning Center for
Earthenware

Boryeong Learning Center for Nampo Ink Stone

Daejeon Daejeon Learning Center for Intangible Cultural Properties

Gyeongsangbuk-do

Hansan Ramie Weaving
Learning Center for
Hansan Ramie Weaving

Geumsan Woodcarving Master

Gyeongju
Stuff Master
Quiver Master

Gimje Ceramic Ware Master

Buan Ceramic
Ware Master / Buan
Learning Center for
National Intangible
Cultural Heritage

Imsil Hanji Paper Master

Sancheong Learning Center for
Sancheong Woodcarving

Gochang Compass Master / Learning Center for Compass

Yangsan Dancheong Master
Buddhistic Drawing Master
Palace Silk Flower Master

Namwon Nickel Tobacco Pipe Master
Learning Center of Nickel Tobacco Pipe Master

Gyeongsangnam-do

Busan Embroidery
Master

Damyang
Colored Bamboo Basket Master
Learning Center for Damyang Bamboo Craft
Learning Center for Damyang Colored Bamboo Basket

Jinju Learning Center
for Pocket Knife

Naju
Naju Saetgol
Fabric Dye Master

Gwangyang Pocket Knife Master
Gwangyang Learning Center for
Pocket Knife

Jeollanam-do

Jade Master
Learning Center for
Mokpo Jade Master
Mokpo

Boseong Bamboo Searing Master

Tongyeong
Najeon Master
Brass Master
Bamboo Screen Master
Tongyeong Learning Center for
Tongyeong Crafts

Jangheung Roof Tile Master

Gangjin
Celadon Ware Master
Earthenware Master

Gokseong Pocket Knife Master
Learning Center of Burned Bamboo Pocket Knife
Small Table Master / Burned Bamboo Pocket Knife
Gokseong / Learning Center for Gokseong Dolsilnai

○ National Intangible Cultural Heritage

● Intangible Cultural Heritage

● Learning Centers for Important
Intangible Cultural Properties

Headband Master / Skullcap Master / Gat Master
Jeju Learning Center for Important Intangible Cultural Properties
Learning Center of Jeju Gat
Jeju

List of Plates

Cover
Celadon *Maebyeong* with Incised Lotus Scroll Design, National Treasure No. 97, Goryeo, 12th century, H. 43.9cm, National Museum of Korea

Bibliography

Historical Literature
Xu Jing, *Xuanhe Fengshi Gaoli Tujing* 宣和奉使高麗圖經 (An Illustrated Account of a Diplomatic Mission to Goryeo in the Xuanhe Period)

Monographs
Choi, Kun et al., *KOREAN ART BOOK: Pottery and Celadon I, II*, Yekyong Publishing, 2000.
Choi, Kun, Ki-hoon Chang, and Jeong-yong Lee, *Baekja: Korean Traditional Porcelain*, Korea Craft & Design Foundation, 2014.
Jeong, Yang-mo, *Goryeo Celadon*, Daewon Publishing, 1998.
Kang, Dae-gyu and Yeong-won Kim, *Ceramic Craft*, Sol Publishing, 2004.
Kang, Min-gi, Suk-hee Yi, Ki-hoon Chang, and Yong-cheol Shin, *Click, History of Korean Art*, Yekyong Publishing, 2011.
Kim, Yun-jeong et al., *Dictionary of Korean Ceramics*, Kyungin Publishing, 2015.
National Institute of Korean History, *Clay of the Korean Peninsula Made into Ceramics*, Kyungin Publishing, 2010.
Quinn, Anthony, *Ceramic Design Course: Principles, Practice, and Techniques: A Complete Course for Ceramicists*, translated by Jin-ho Im and Se-eun Kim, Mijin Publisher, 2009.
Shiraki, Yoichi, *Dictionary of Pottery Arts and Ceramics*, Gihodo Books, 1982.
The Special Committee for the Virtual Museum of Korean History, *Goryeo Dynasty I*, Sakyejul Publishing, 2002.

Catalogues
Jeonju National Museum, *Fine Art of Jeollabuk-do*, 2009.
National Museum of Korea, *The Best Under Heaven: The Celadons of Korea*, 2012.
National Museum of Korea, *The Royal Ceramics of Goryeo Dynasty*, 2008.

Research Papers
Baek, Eun-gyeong, "A Study on the Sanghyeong Celadon of the Goryeo Dynasty," Master's Thesis, Hongik University, 2004.
Jang, Nam-won, "A Study on the Celadon of the Mid-Goryeo Dynasty," Ph.D. Dissertation, Ewha Womans University, 2002.
Kang, Gyung-in, "The Kiln Structures and Color Changes of Goryeo Celadon," *Characteristics of Colors in Goryeo Celadon*, Goryeo Celadon Museum, 2010.
Yi, Jong-min, "A Study on the Early Celadon of Korea," Ph.D. Dissertation, Hongik University, 2002.

Websites
Cultural Heritage Administration   www.cha.go.kr
Gansong Art Museum   kansong.org
Goryeo Celadon Museum   www.celadon.go.kr
Haegang Ceramics Museum   www.haegang.org
Horim Museum   www.horimmuseum.org
Korea Ceramic Foundation   www.kocef.org
Leeum, Samsung Museum of Art   leeum.samsungfoundation.org
National Museum of Korea   www.museum.go.kr
National Research Institute of Maritime Cultural Heritage   www.seamuse.go.kr

Collaborators

Individuals
Bang Seung-hyeong (Goryeo Celadon Museum)
Choi In-kyu (Jangwhiyo)
Han Jin-wu (Goryeo Celadon Museum)
Jo Ju-il (Goryeo Celadon Museum)
Jo Se-yeon (Bogwangyo)
Jo You-bok (Goryeo Celadon Museum)
Kim Bok-han (Hancheong doyo)
Kim Hyeon-wuk (Hangcheong doyo)
Kim Jong-ho (Songwolyo)
Kim Pan-ki (Jignag doyo)
Kim Se-yong (Sechang Art Ceramic Research Institute)
Kim Sung-tae (Songwolyo)
Kim Yu-sung (Towu gongbang)
Kwon Tae-hyun (Hyocheonyo)
Lee Dong-ha (Dept. of Ceramic Art, Hanyang Women's University)
Lee Eun-bum
Lee Ka-jin
Ma Gwang-won (Goryeo Celadon Museum)
Wi Seong-gon (Goryeo Celadon Museum)
Yang Myung-hwan (Cheongjinyo)
Yoo Kwang-yul (Haegangyo)
Yun Min-hui (Goryeo Celadon Museum)

Organizations
Bogwangyo
Cheongjinyo
Cultural Heritage Administration
Goryeo Celadon Museum
Haegang Ceramics Museum
Haegang Institute of Koryo Celadon
Haegangyo
Hancheong doyo
Horim Museum
Hyocheonyo
Janghwi Koryo Celadon
Jangwhiyo
Jigang doyo
Kansong Museum
Korea Ceramic Foundation
Leeum, Samsung Museum of Art
National Museum of Korea
National Research Institute of Maritime Cultural Heritage
Samsung Foundation of Culture
Sechang Art Ceramic Research Institute
Songwolyo
Towu gongbang
Yanggu Porcelain Museum

Index

Korean Craft & Design Resource Book 12

Cheongja: Korean Traditional Celadon

Writers
Kwon So-hyun (Associate Curator, Jeonju National Museum)
Kang Gyung-in (Research Director, Goryeo Celadon Museum)
Seo Jeong-gurl (CEO, Korea Ceramic Foundation)

Advisors
Jang Nam-won (Associate Professor & Museum Director, Dept. of Art History, Ewha Womans University)
Kim Yun-jeong (Professor, Division of Cultural Heritage Convergence, Korea University)

Korean-English Translator
Park Shin-hee (Jangtongbang)

Translation Supervisor
Chang Ki-hoon (Director, Gyeonggi Ceramic Museum)

Process Management
Hong Ki-hye (Team Manager, Korea Craft & Design Foundation)
Jeon Min-kyeong (Senior Researcher, Korea Craft & Design Foundation)

Editing & Design & Layout
Mijin Publisher

Photographers
Seo Heun-gang
Seon Yu-min

Publisher
Choi Bong-hyun (President, Korea Craft & Design Foundation)

Korea Craft & Design Foundation
KCDF Gallery, 8 Insa-dong 11-gil, Jongno-gu, Seoul, Korea
5F Haeyoung Bldg., 53 Yulgok-ro, Jongno-gu, Seoul, Korea
phone: 82-2-398-7900 fax: 82-2-398-7999
www.kcdf.kr

First published on December 29, 2017

ISBN 978-89-97252-91-6(04630)
ISBN 978-89-97252-13-8 (set)

16,000 KRW